# CITY ON FIRE

## KINGSTON UPON HULL 1939–45

## NICK COOPER

AMBERLEY

*For my maternal grandparents, who lived and worked in,
and sailed from Kingston upon Hull during the war.*

*For my mother, born in the city in 1942.*

*For my father, who sadly did not live to read this book.*

*For my wife, who supported me in the writing of it.*

*For my daughter, who was born while it was being written.*

First published 2017

Amberley Publishing
The Hill, Stroud
Gloucestershire, GL5 4EP

www.amberley-books.com

Copyright © Nick Cooper, 2017

The right of Nick Cooper to be identified as the Author
of this work has been asserted in accordance with the
Copyrights, Designs and Patents Act 1988.

British Library Cataloguing in Publication Data.
A catalogue record for this book is available from the British Library.

ISBN 978 1 4456 7204 5 (print)
ISBN 978 1 4456 7205 2 (ebook)

Origination by Amberley Publishing.
Printed in Great Britain.

# Contents

# Chapter 1

# A City Apart

Towards the end of the twelfth century, the monks of Meaux Abbey, to the east of Beverley, needed a port through which to export the wool produced on their lands. For this they chose a spot on the west bank of the River Hull, where it flowed into the wide Humber Estuary, 30 miles from the sea. They named the settlement Wyke upon Hull, but in 1293 King Edward I was so impressed by its potential that he bought it from the Abbey, granted it a town charter on 1 April 1299, and renamed it King's Town upon Hull.

Under this royal patronage Hull flourished, both as a port and a regional centre, which became inextricably entwined with the fortunes of the family of William de la Pole. A wealthy wool merchant, he organised the loans which allowed the resumption in 1327 of the English military campaign against Scotland by Queen Isabella and Roger Mortimer, regents for the boy King Edward III. In return, de la Pole was granted valuable trading concessions, he was knighted, and he became Hull's first Lord Mayor.

Hull was given permission to fortify itself around the same time, and by 1356 a wall enclosed the whole town on the west of the River Hull, which was all the more necessary given that, as a legacy of the Scottish Wars, Hull had become an important regional store for arms and ammunition – a tempting prize for any force in need of both. This proved the case in 1536, when Hull refused to join the 'Pilgrimage of Grace', the Yorkshire rebellion against King Henry VIII's schism with the Roman Catholic Church.

When Henry and his fifth wife, Catherine Howard, visited the town five years later, he instructed that the fortifications be expanded, especially on the east side of the River Hull. This eventually led to the conversion of the De La Pole house into the castle at the centre of a wall running parallel to the river, at either end of which was a large Blockhouse. In the meantime, the King was so impressed by the reception they received in Hull that he gifted the town with his own sword, but nearly a century later one of his successors was made less welcome.

On the eve of the English Civil War, Hull was largely Royalist in temperament, so in January 1642 Parliament despatched Sir John Hotham to take over as governor, in order to prevent the stockpile of munitions falling into King Charles' hands. Having previously camped at Beverley with 300 loyal cavaliers, the King rode to Hull on 23 April – St George's Day – no doubt counting on the inherent patriotism of the day to work in his favour, but instead found the gates of Hull barred to him. From the ramparts Hotham apologised and begged forgiveness, but steadfastly refused the King entry. Denouncing him as a traitor, Charles seethed outside the walls for some five hours before giving up and returning to Beverley.

Hotham then tried to backtrack, conspiring to surrender Hull to Charles in 1643, quickly dissipating any lingering Royalist sympathies in the city, and the population invited Lord Ferdinando Fairfax to replace Hotham (who was eventually hanged for treason at Tyburn) as governor. This prompted a six-week siege by Royalist forces, which the Parliamentarians and townspeople together successfully resisted. Hull, it could be said, was developing a habit

4

The fortified town of Hull in 1610.

of choosing its own allegiances, and could not be taken for granted. After the Civil War the fortifications were remodelled, with the castle and south blockhouse forming the basis of an artillery fort known as the Citadel.

Since the days of the Meaux Abbey monks, the tidal River Hull was used as the city's natural harbour, with a series of crowded wharves and warehouses on the west bank, which became known as the Haven. By the late eighteenth century it was clear that the facilities were becoming increasingly inadequate. In 1775, construction began on a 10-acre (4 hectare) artificial dock on the west side of the River Hull, principally on the site of the now redundant north wall of the Old Town. The entrance to what initially became known as simply The Dock – later Queen's Dock – was some 1,200 yards (1,100m) from where the river met the Humber, and it opened in September 1778.

The original dock had barely opened before there were calls for further expansion, which eventually manifested as Humber Dock. Built along the line of the town ditch or moat, its entrance was on the Humber itself, some 330 yards (300m) to the west of the mouth of the Hull, and it opened in June 1809. Once trade had increased enough to justify it, the existing docks were linked by a third, Junction Dock – later Prince's Dock – which opened in 1829.

It was into a family that had prospered thanks to Hull's role as a port that the city's greatest son was born in 1759. Aged just 21, William Wilberforce was elected as Hull's independent Member of Parliament in 1780, a post he took seriously, while still enjoying what would now be called a playboy lifestyle. This changed in 1785, when he underwent an Evangelical Christian conversion, and 1787 he agreed to take up in Parliament the cause of those seeking to abolish the transatlantic slave trade, 'provided that no person more proper could be found'. It was a battle that would occupy Wilberforce for the rest of his life, culminating in the Slave Trade Act of 1807, which not only abolished the trade within the British Empire, but also precipitated the Royal Navy actively suppressing the trade by other nations. The institution of slavery itself was outlawed by the Slavery Abolition Act of 1833, passed by Parliament three days before Wilberforce's death, and came into force the following year.

The railway came to Hull in 1840 when the Hull & Barnsley Railway (H&BR) opened, with the mixed goods and passenger Manor House Street terminus station on the west side of Humber Dock. This precipitated the construction of the aptly named Railway Dock, to the north of and parallel to the railway tracks, and connected to the west side of Prince's Dock. The H&BR added a new north-eastern branch to Bridlington – via Cottingham, Beverley, and Driffield – in 1846, and two years later the company opened a new passenger terminus. This took its name from the nearby Paragon Street, although some were subsequently apt to suggest that it hinted at delusions of grandeur, either by the railway company or the city itself!

Construction of the first dock on the east side of the River Hull, on land to the east of the Citadel – with connections to both the Hull and the Humber – began in 1845, and it opened as

By 1817 Humber Dock had been completed, and the Citadel built to protect the town.

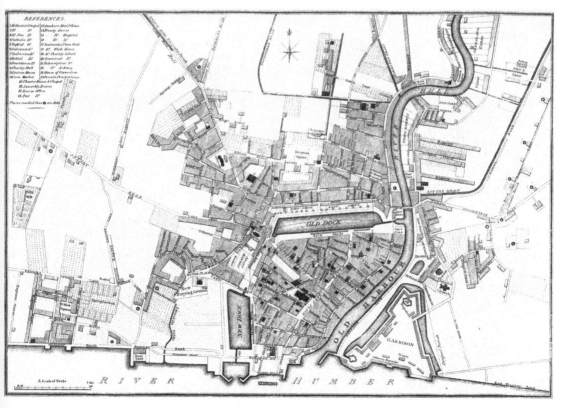

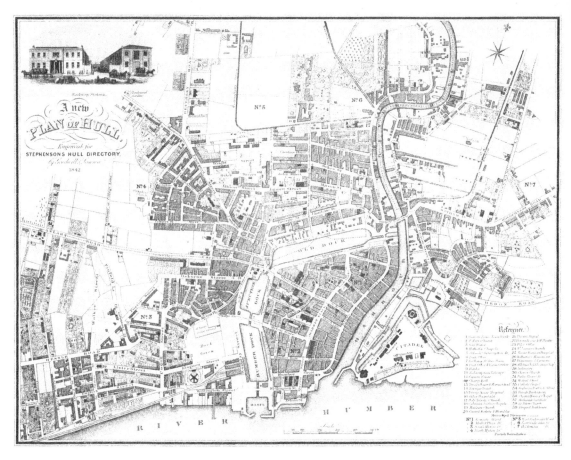

After twenty-five years of rapid expansion, the railway station shown in the top left inset is the one adjacent to Humber Dock.

Victoria Dock in 1850. During the remaining decades of the century further docks were added along the banks of the Humber on both the west (St Andrew's, William Wright and Albert Docks) and east (Alexandra Dock) sides of the Hull, often involving part-reclamation of the foreshore.

In 1885, new railway connections were provided by the North Eastern Railway (NER), whose line approached from the west through Spring Bank, where it split, with one branch ending in Neptune Street Goods station next to Albert Dock, and the other curving round the then outskirts of the city to the Cannon Street terminus station. Another branch crossed the River Hull and terminated at the NER's own Alexandra Dock.

The last major dock to be built was Joint Dock, so named as it was a collaboration between the NER and the H&BR. When built between 1906 and 1914, it was roughly T-shaped, with the base connected to the Humber by a long channel. Upon opening it was named King George Dock. Construction involved extensive foreshore reclamation, with space reserved for future extensions, the first of which was added to the south-west after the First World War.[1]

By the start of the twentieth century the city was truly girdled by railway track, with eight passenger stations, fifteen goods stations, and numerous sidings and depots. The grouping of the nation's railway companies in the 1920s brought all of Hull's lines under the control of the new London & North Eastern Railway (LNER). The old NER Cannon Street station was relegated to freight use only, while some of the smaller passenger stations closed completely. Despite this, passengers could travel west to Doncaster and Leeds, north to

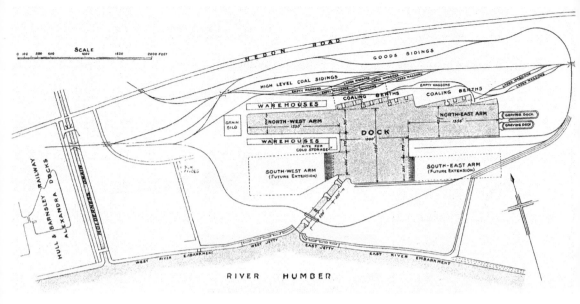

Plan of the intended Hull Joint Dock, later King George Dock. The south-western extension was completed to a different outline before the Second World War. (Author's collection)

A contemporary artist's impression of the Joint Dock under construction. (Author's collection)

Bridlington and Scarborough, or west to Hornsea or Withernsea, but the Humber was an obvious and insurmountable barrier to the south.

The existence of a ferry between Hull and North Lincolnshire dated back to Roman times and for centuries such a journey by sail and oar was perilous, to say the least. Those who risked it for the sake of avoiding the long way round by land could leave in fine weather, but were at the mercy of the elements changing before those conveying them – for all their skill, knowledge and strength – could deliver them intact to the other side of the estuary.

The advent of steam paddleships quickened and regulated the ferry traffic, and, inevitably, the main service was taken over by a railway company seeking to establish a cross-Humber link, specifically the Manchester, Sheffield and Lincolnshire Railway. In 1848, they bought out the existing ferries and constructed a new pier at New Holland to service them. Stretching 1,370ft

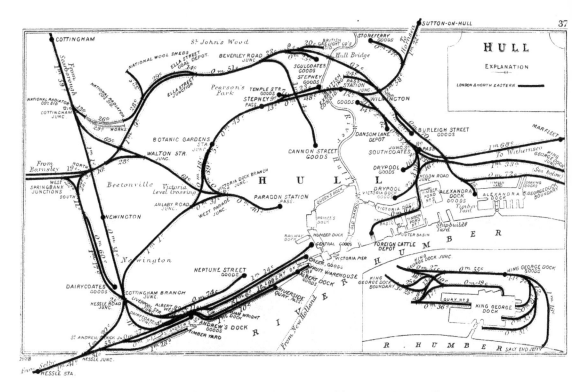

Railways in Hull following the pre-war amalgamation of lines. (Author's collection)

(418m) into the Humber, it was substantial enough to carry a double railway track all the way to a small station at its head, which opened in 1849.[2] On one side of the tracks there was a raised walkway for foot passengers, and on the other a vehicle roadway. This was in imperfect solution, because once passengers had made the journey from New Holland to Hull, those wishing to travel onwards still had to journey by foot, cart or coach to either Paragon or Cannon Street stations.

As the years passed the ferry traffic grew, and increases in the size of rolling stock resulted in the conversion of the pier to single-track working only. In 1922, work was started to strengthen the wooden pier with additional steel supports,[3] renovations that were not completed until 1928. Around the same time it was becoming clear that the paddle ferries in use at the time – the *Cleethorpes* (1903), *Brocklesby* (1912), and *Killingholme* (1912) – were struggling to accommodate the numbers of passengers and motor vehicles. By then control of the ferry service had passed to the LNER, which commissioned two new vessels, the *Tattershall Castle* and the *Wingfield Castle*. They entered service in 1934, after which the *Cleethorpes* and *Brocklesby* were retired. A refined version of the new vessels, the *Lincoln Castle*, would join the fleet in 1940.

By the beginning of the twentieth century, Hull was the largest fishing port in the country, if not the world, and by the outbreak of the Second World War it was reckoned that around 60,000 of the 330,000 population (18 per cent) were involved in the fishing industry in one way or another.[4] For the trawlermen themselves, their work was hard and dangerous enough in peacetime, but war made it more so. During the First World War most trawlers had to ply their normal trade with the additional threat from German surface warships and U-boats, yet perhaps one of the more notorious incidents occurred during a conflict in which Britain took no part.

War had broken out between Russia and Japan in early 1904, and in October of that year warships of the Russian Baltic Fleet were despatched to reinforce the 1st Pacific Squadron.

A precarious landing for the Humber ferry at New Holland in 1948, as the new pier in the background nears completion. (David Hall McKewan, 1816–1873; author's collection)

The Hull Corporation ferry pier, shown here between the wars. (Author's collection)

The intended route took them through the North Sea and the English Channel, thousands of miles from enemy territory, but rumours were rife that Japanese vessels were nearby.

On the evening of 21 October, traversing the Dogger Bank, Russian lookouts reported a large number of small vessels ahead of them, supposedly approaching in formation. The panicked Russian officers misidentified the ships as Japanese torpedo boats, and opened fire at what was actually a fleet of Hull trawlers. The *Crane* was sunk, with the loss of her first officer and mate; four other trawlers were damaged and six crewmen injured, one mortally. In the confusion two Russian cruisers were targeted by their own side, with the loss of one sailor and a chaplain. It took twenty minutes for the Russians to realise their mistake, and the only thing that prevented greater bloodshed was their exceptionally poor gunnery.

The battered trawlers limped home, reaching Hull on 23 October and breaking the news of what was quickly dubbed the 'Russian Outrage'. Messages of condolence to the city – including the King himself – were swiftly issued, and a deputation of survivors were whisked to London to brief the Foreign Office and other officials. One man brought with him a fragment of Russian shell, and when another was asked for any similar physical evidence, he stated bluntly:

There are two headless trunks at Hull. Several men have been struck, and some crippled, at least one good trawler has been sent to the bottom, and the facts speak eloquently for themselves.[5]

A contemporary artist's impression of the Russian attack on the Hull fishing fleet in 1904. (Author's collection)

Damage to one of the Hull trawlers. (Author's collection)

Another witness said:

> The reason for the [Russian] firing is beyond my comprehension... They gave us no warning whatsoever. They were not near enough to speak to us. Our men, of course, are boiling with indignation at this cowardly and unprovoked attack upon us.

Hull now found itself caught up in the maelstrom of the First World War. As well as the obvious contributions to the war effort of the Merchant Navy, thousands of Hull men and women volunteered or were later conscripted into the armed forces. Five 'service' or 'Pals' battalions of the East Yorkshire Regiment were raised in the city, and, along with the regular and territorial battalions, served on the Western Front, in the Middle East and at Gallipoli.

Although the German fleet shelled Hartlepool, Whitby and Scarborough in December 1914, it never dared to enter the Humber, let alone approach Hull, due in no small part to the defences of the estuary. These included two sea forts on Bull Sands and Haile Sands off the coasts of Spurn Head, and the Lincolnshire coast, respectively, but the city was not immune to a new form of attack.

Just six years before war broke out, the author H.G. Wells speculated on the effect that aircraft would inevitably have on modern warfare in his novel *The War in the Air*. In it the aptly named Bert Smallways, an unassuming bicycle shop assistant, finds himself at the centre of a conflict, which sees New York attacked and largely destroyed by airships and heavier-than-air aircraft.

Airships of both the German Navy and Army first began to mount raids on the UK in January 1915, when two Zeppelins failed to reach the Humber area and attacked Great Yarmouth instead. Hull was successfully targeted in later raids (see Chapter 2). After the war a cenotaph was constructed in Paragon Square, forming a sombre backdrop to an earlier Boer War memorial in the same location.

The Telegraph Act of 1899 allowed local authorities to operate their own telephone systems in the same way as other utilities (electricity, gas, water, etc.). Thirteen municipalities were granted licences, of which six actually started services. Hull was the last to do so in 1904, with an exchange opening in the former Trippett Street public baths. Ten years later, when the licence came up for renewal, Hull was the last municipal telephone system standing, with the rest having been subsumed into the General Post Office's (GPO) near monopoly. The licence was renewed, subject to the Corporation buying out the remaining assets of the National Telephone Company (taken over by the GPO elsewhere) in the city, which it successfully did.

The Corporation's Telephone Department was quick to keep pace with developments in technology, but did not feel the need to reinvent the wheel. When the GPO introduced its iconic red K6 telephone kiosk in 1936, Hull also bought its iconic red K6 telephone kiosks, ground off the Royal crowns, and painted them a smart white and green livery. Later acquisitions were made without the crowns in the first place, and the green part of the colour scheme dropped, but to this day Hull is a landscape of white telephone kiosks.

Despite Hull's overriding connection with the sea, it was not devoid of aviation. Leeds-born Robert Blackburn formed the Blackburn Aeroplane & Motor Company in 1914, and five years later built a factory at Brough, the location on the bank of the Humber facilitating seaplane production. The village's modest railway station was expanded to cope with the thousands of workers who commuted from Hull every day.[6]

More well-known outside the city are the exploits of the aviation pioneer Amy Johnson. The daughter of a fish merchant, Johnson took up flying as a hobby while working as a legal secretary, and qualified as both a pilot and a ground engineer in 1929. She then bought a second-hand de Havilland Gipsy Moth biplane – which she named *Jason* – and in 1930 became the first woman to fly solo from the UK to Australia. Numerous other firsts – both solo and with a co-pilot – followed. In 1932, she married fellow pilot Jim Mollinson. The press dubbed them 'the flying sweethearts', but the relationship could appropriately be described as turbulent, ending in divorce in 1938.

Although inevitably battered by the Great Depression of the 1930s, Hull did not stagnate. Slums in the centre of the city were cleared in the 1920s and '30s, with the occupants moved out to well-planned and well-built municipal housing estates in the west, north, and east. The Corporation also invested in the city's cultural life, opening the Museum of Commerce and Transport on the High Street in 1925, the Railway Museum on Paragon Street in 1933, and in 1935 the redundant Queen's Dock was filled in and turned into Queen's Gardens. In 1927, the industrialist Thomas Ferens gifted a public art gallery to the city.

The Corporation had previously bought Wilberforce House in 1903, opening it as a museum in 1906.[7] In 1933, to celebrate the centenary of his death, a new exhibit was added: a waxwork of William Wilberforce himself – a gift from Madame Tussauds – shown at his desk. In 1941, even as Hull was enduring German air raids, an architectural guidebook noted of the tableaux:

> It is delightful; so real does he seem that we almost expect him to rise from his chair and plead once more for the slaves who remain in the world, five million strong over a hundred years after, and, as we write, a hundred million more enslaved in Nazi chains.[8]

Paragon Square in the 1930s. (Author's collection)

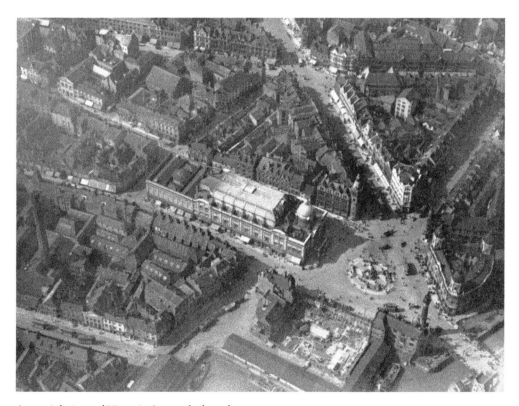

An aerial view of Victoria Square before the war.

# Chapter 2
# Prelude

In January 1915, at the height of the First World War, German airships crossed the English Channel for the first time in order to bomb the UK. Although they flew high enough to avoid anti-aircraft fire from the ground, they were susceptible to bad weather and imprecise navigation. Despite this, between June 1915 and August 1918, Zeppelins located and bombed Hull on no less than eight occasions, inflicting unimaginable damage and resulting in civilian casualties. One of the raids saw the destruction of many commercial and residential properties in the immediate vicinity of the Medieval Holy Trinity Church,[1] which itself was largely untouched. Picture postcards sold after the attack showed Hull's great church standing defiantly amidst the surrounding devastation.

Hull weathered the storm of its first Blitz, although the civil defence measures meeting it were an inevitable mix of ad hoc improvisation and chance luck, with many headaches for

Holy Trinity Church untouched amid the destruction of a Zeppelin raid during the First World War. (Author's collection)

the Corporation. While Londoners could retreat to the relative safety of the Underground railway, Hull's population was ill-protected. Some were able to arrange construction of their own air-raid shelters, but for many the only option was to walk out of the city and into the surrounding countryside at night. Such 'trekking' caused many problems for the authorities, not least because of the obvious risk of large numbers of people – many encumbered by prized possessions they did not wish to leave at home – venturing out in the blackout to areas ill-equipped to receive them, even temporarily.

Towards the end of 1916 and into 1917, German tactics changed to the use of Gotha G.IV & G.V bombers, which were limited in their bomb-load, but were more precise. British attempts to shoot down the bombers were largely ineffectual, with most fighters being unable to climb high enough to engage them, and with falling anti-aircraft shells being reckoned to cause as much damage as the enemy bombs.

Throughout the 1920s and early '30s, tactical bombing was used on a minor scale in various colonial conflicts – most notably by the British in Iraq – while theories of strategic bombing were developed by a number of the Western powers. At the same time, the evolution of the bomber was resulting in aircraft with ever increasing bomb-loads, range and speed, but which were vulnerable to attack by enemy fighters. To counter this, defensive armament was increased to such a degree that it became widely held that concentrated bomber formations could effectively hold off such attacks, and thus the majority would reach their target. In this context it was believed that a single 'super-raid' could effectively obliterate a city in a very short space of time.

Speaking to Parliament in November 1932, the Conservative MP Stanley Baldwin warned:

> I think it is well also for the man in the street to realise that there is no power on earth that can protect him from being bombed, whatever people may tell him. The bomber will always get through, and it is very easy to understand that if you realise the area of space. Take any large town you like in this island or on the Continent within the reach of an aerodrome. For the defence of that town and its suburbs you have to split the air into sectors for defence. Calculate that the bombing aeroplanes will be at least 20,000ft. in the air, and perhaps higher, and it is a matter of mathematical calculation that you will have sectors of from 10 to hundreds of cubic miles. Imagine 100 cubic miles covered with cloud and fog, and you can calculate how many aeroplanes you would have to throw into that to have much chance of catching odd [bomber] aeroplanes as they fly through it.[2]

Coupled with these fears was a concern that if deep air-raid shelters were constructed and actually used, many people would develop a 'deep shelter mentality' and refuse to come back up again. If everything they needed was below ground, they might forgo their jobs on the surface, even if they were vital to the war effort.

In 1934, the flamboyant producer Alexander Korda managed to persuade H.G. Wells to adapt his 1933 novel *The Shape of Things to Come* for the cinema screen. The film shows the fictional city of Everytown passing through three phases of future history: a surprise air attack by an unnamed enemy country on Christmas Eve 1940; the descent of the world into primitive medievalism in the late-1960s; and finally a scientific and technological rebirth in the twenty-first century. The city is a clear stand-in for London, but in typical Wellsian fashion the metaphorical name of 'Everytown' made clear that it represented *all* large British towns and cities and their vulnerability to aerial attack. Perhaps surprisingly, the first British screening of the film outside London was in Hull in July 1936.[3]

Although *The Shape of Things to Come* was fiction, the outbreak of the Spanish Civil War in July 1936 soon saw civilian populations attacked by modern bombers for real. Even before the infamous raid on Guernica in 1937, German *Legion Condor* and Italian *Aviazione Legionaria* bombers – supporting General Franco's fascist rebels – attacked the besieged

Scenes predicting an aerial attack on a British city in *Things to Come* (1936). (Author's collection)

capital of Madrid in November 1936. An English-language[4] poster produced by the Spanish Republican government to raise awareness and support abroad was headed: 'MADRID – THE "MILITARY" PRACTICE OF THE REBELS', above a mortuary photograph of the body of a child killed in one raid, and the stark warning: 'IF YOU TOLERATE THIS, YOUR CHILDREN WILL BE NEXT.'[5]

During a period of just under 48 hours from 16–18 March 1938, the *Aviazione Legionaria* carried out thirteen air raids against the Spanish government-held city of Barcelona. Several months later, the British war correspondent John Langdon-Davies' published account of the attack suggested that it amounted to a deliberate and systematic experiment in the aerial bombardment of a civilian population, in preparation for a future conflict against Britain. The three crucial factors were the varying times between each raid, the aircraft gliding in from high altitude with their engines off, and the use of large capacity high explosive bombs (HEs).

Often, the first the government forces knew of an attack was the bombs themselves exploding, so the single-note air-raid sirens only sounded *after* this had happened. Coupled with varying the time between raids, this provoked extreme anxiety and confusion in the population, who could not know when the next attack would occur, or even whether one had started or finished. Meanwhile, the use of higher capacity bombs than had been dropped on the city previously showed how much more effective they were in destroying urban targets. Earlier raids had been limited to bombs in the 50-100kg range; the March 1938 raids involved 250kg and 500kg bombs, which had a wider blast radius, and produced a secondary 'suction' effect – after the initial outward blast – that literally pulled the front off nearby buildings.

Langdon-Davies was critical of contemporary British Air Raid Precautions (ARP), and in particular the heavy emphasis on the threat of poison gas, which, although available, had not been used in Spain, supposedly on moral grounds. More importantly, the use of high explosive bombs made a mockery of the idea that ordinary people could construct – and survive in – gas-proof rooms in their own homes. Instead he advocated the construction of large purpose-built gas- and blast-proof public shelters.[6]

In pushing for improvements in ARP, Langdon-Davies was by no means a lone voice, with his most well-known fellow critic being the geneticist Professor J.B.S. Haldane, whose own book on the subject appeared at the same time. He also drew heavily on events in Spain – including his own experience of an air raid whilst there – and was generally in agreement with Langdon-Davies on many points, although he was highly sceptical that gas would ever be used en masse against civilian targets, more for reasons of practicality than morality.[7]

While Langdon-Davies was preoccupied with a 'super-raid' on London, Haldane's scope was wider, and he was mindful of Hull's unique position in a number of ways. He noted that while a blackout could be effective, 'certain towns, particularly London, Hull, and Edinburgh, are near conspicuous landmarks on the coast, and would hardly be missed.'[8] On the subject of civilian evacuation, he stated that it should apply to, 'Children of school age from all large towns considered vulnerable (e.g. London and Hull certainly, Sheffield and Birmingham probably, Glasgow and Cardiff doubtfully).'[9]

Naturally enough, Germany made extensive plans to bomb targets within the UK. Pre-war commercial aerial photographs were augmented with clandestine reconnaissance by scheduled Lufthansa flights, along with Luftwaffe incursions at the start of the war. These photographs were arranged to show targets from different approach angles, with specific locations highlighted for the benefit of navigators and bomb-aimers. For Hull, the targeting information ran to a full eleven pages, with East Park, West Park, and Queen's Gardens (dubbed 'Zentralpark' or 'Central Park') as orientation features. From the air the sheer number of targets within the city – and particularly along the banks of both the Humber and the Hull – was glaringly apparent.[10]

German planners also appropriated standard Ordnance Survey maps, re-scaling and reprinting them in order to be overlaid with targeting information. Principal railway sites, docks, industries and other infrastructure were highlighted with colour-coding and symbols denoting their exact nature. Locations in Hull to actively avoid were few and far between, although the Royal Infirmary on Prospect Street and some – but not all – other hospitals were indicated by the ubiquitous red cross.[11]

In late September 1938, at the height of the Munich Crisis, while Prime Minister Neville Chamberlain negotiated with Hitler, ARP measures were activated throughout the UK. Civilian gas masks were distributed, and it was reported on 22 September that around half of the 300,000 earmarked for Hull were already in the city, with more being delivered for assembly and distribution. A snap census was organised so that the local authorities could determine how many and of what size respirators should be delivered to each home.[12]

Appeals were made for the recruitment of both ARP volunteers and police Special Constables, although neither was very successful.[13] By 23 September only around 100 of the required 2,500 Specials had volunteered,[14] and the following day just 600 of the 4,000 ARP workers needed had come forwards.[15] The city was divided into four ARP Divisions, and

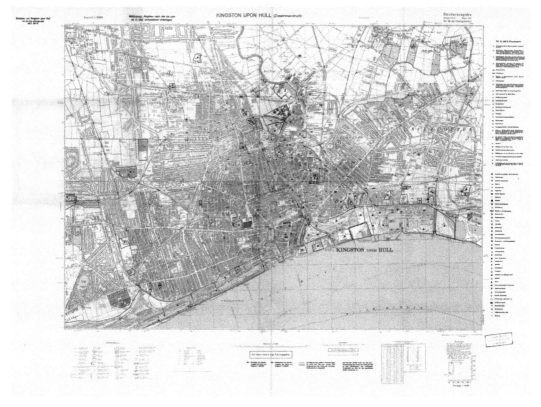

A German appropriated Ordnance Survey map showing targets in Hull. (Author's collection)

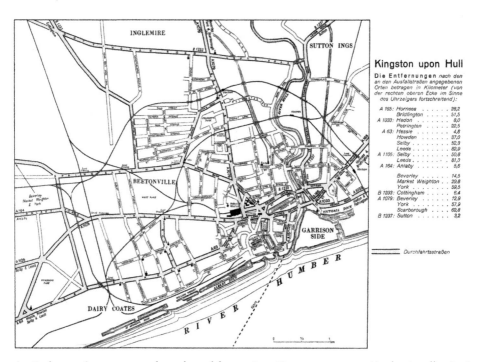

An Ordnance Survey street plan adapted for use in a German gazetteer. (Author's collection)

then into twenty-nine smaller Areas, with the boundaries of many being the railway lines as natural obstacles.[16] The local ARP Committee made a request that vacant land be made available for the construction of air-raid defences – initially trenches – but it was hoped that more substantial shelters could be constructed, and work began almost immediately in Queen's Gardens on protection for city-centre workers.[17]

At a lively Left Book Club meeting on 25 September at the Hull Royal Institution on Albion Street, attended by Professor Haldane, Alderman J.L. (Leo) Schultz made the rather hasty promise that:

> Very probably, every citizen of Hull will be protected by bomb-proof shelters, such as have been outlined by Professor Haldane, and they will be provided at such speed as Professor Haldane has indicated as possible. In spite of what the Government is not doing, it has been announced that the City Council of Hull are going to protect the people of Hull, and we intend to do it.[18]

He was quick to point out, however, that this didn't mean deep tunnels, but rather shallow or surface shelters, and that the brunt of the cost would fall on Hull ratepayers, rather than the government.

Haldane himself was sure that Hull would be a priority target, but thought that only high explosive and larger incendiary bombs (IBs) would be used. He rejected the suggestion that these were not possible in Hull due to the high water table, but dismissed the then popular idea of a Humber Tunnel that could double as a refuge, as access would be too limited in an emergency.[19]

He also stressed the need for the early evacuation of children:

> I believe you could get every schoolchild in Hull out within a very few hours, providing you used buses and other large vehicles, and organised the evacuation so as to avoid traffic blocks. There is a fair amount of country behind Hull, and it ought to be possible for the Council, in conjunction with the teachers, to draw up an evacuation plan. And remember that 50 children in an isolated barn are safer, if less comfortable, than in a group of cottages which might make a target.[20]

The main delivery of gas masks started on 28 September, and Corporation contractors started work on garden shelters for every homeowner who did not value their lawn over their family's safety.[21] A test of the air-raid siren or 'buzzer' used during the First World War was carried out at 15:00 on the 29th, but was less than satisfactory. Installed on the Hull Electricity Undertaking on Sculcoates Lane, the buzzer had been hastily retrieved from the Corporation's Museum Department and may not have been installed correctly. Although it could be heard in some districts, it was virtually inaudible in others, necessitating hasty adjustments and a re-test a week later.[22]

Having reached an agreement with Adolf Hitler, Benito Mussolini, and French Premier Édouard Daladier, Prime Minister Neville Chamberlain returned to Britain. After his aircraft landed at Heston Aerodrome on 30 September, he promised 'peace for our time' publicly, whilst privately hoping he had bought the nation vital time to re-arm. Britain would not be ready to fight Germany in 1939, but it would be more ready than it had been in 1938. Having secured the largely German-speaking Sudetenland from Czechoslovakia by negotiation, Hitler would wait barely six months before taking the rest of the country by force.

In the meantime, as the country breathed a sigh of relief, Hull had a timely opportunity to relax and enjoy a hopeful peace at the annual fair. The event dated back to the days of the Meaux Abbey monks' control of Wyke upon Hull, and was first held in 1278. The idea was continued by Edward I, who in 1293 granted a royal charter for an annual fair, and this tradition continued with some variation of duration and date until being finally fixed in 1751 as eleven days from 11 October each year, subsequently reduced to eight days.[23]

The 1938 fair was opened with the usual civic pageantry. The Lord Mayor, Alderman F. Holmes, and numerous dignitaries left the Guildhall at 11 a.m. for the opening ceremony at the 13-acre fairground on Walton Street. Presiding over the ceremony, the chairman of the Markets Committee, Alderman G.E. Farmery said, 'It is indeed a great pleasure to take part in this opening ceremony of Hull's historic fair.' He went on to say something of the history of the event, but with typical Hull reticence noted, 'I will not enter into the debate as to which is the largest fair,' even though pretty much everyone present was assured of the city's claim that theirs was the biggest in the country. In closing, he said, 'This is a fair which appeals to young and old. Thousands visit the fair every year, and I am sure that we are justified in thinking it is a great asset to our city.'[24]

The following day the *Hull Daily Mail* was more forthright, acknowledging just why that year's event was different from recent ones:

> Hull Fair – England's largest pleasure carnival – is always looked forward to with great eagerness by people of all ages, but this year it should be doubly welcomed, falling as it does immediately after the international crisis which brought in its train strain and nervous tension for everyone. It is in events such as Hull Fair which make folk forget their cares and worries and the need for such a tonic was never more opportune.[25]

Nobody knew it at the time, but it was to be the last Hull Fair for six years.

Throughout the last months of 1938 and the first of 1939, the steady stream of recruits for ARP Wardens and Special Constables continued, as did those for the nascent Auxiliary Fire Service (AFS). Firewatchers were raised by neighbourhoods, private business and the public sector. When the time came – and by now it was clear it would – an army of men and women would be prepared to deal with everything Hitler could throw at their city. Or die trying.

Shaken out of complacency, the government set in motion the expansion of the country's defences in anticipation of a Second World War. One of the most tangible of these was the formation of RAF Balloon Command, responsible for the huge tethered barrage balloons that were expected to be a key part of the defence against aerial attack. The barrage for Hull and the Humber was the responsibility of 17 Balloon Centre, which was formed at Hull in January 1939, before moving to a purpose-built site at Sutton-on-Hull, which at the time was still largely farmland.[26] The active defence of the city fell largely to the heavy batteries of the 39th Anti-Aircraft Brigade, Royal Artillery, based at Wenlock Barracks on Anlaby Road.

Wenlock Barracks, the wartime home of 39th Anti-Aircraft Brigade, Royal Artillery, which is still in army use today. (Courtesy of Barnaby Cooper)

Away from these more visible defences, however, measures were being taken to protect the city in a more clandestine way. In January 1937, accompanied by an RAF colleague, Captain P.G. Calvert-Jones paid a visit to Alexander Korda at Denham, Buckinghamshire, where some parts of *The Shape of Things to Come* had been shot, and where he subsequently built a film studio. Korda was keen to form some sort of volunteer defence unit – possibly anti-aircraft or searchlights – amongst his permanent staff of around 1,350 people. In his report, however, Calvert-Jones suggested another possibility:

> The staff employees, buildings and workshops are admirably suited to a Camouflage Unit, if such a unit is required. These men are specialists at 'make believe' and deception in defeating both the eye and the camera. They possess the workmen, material and shops to build jerry constructions for deception purposes. They are in a sense mobile, as most employees arrive and depart by motor-car. Even their 2,000 lights might be used in floodlighting empty fields to resemble aerodromes.[27]

From this idea grew one of the most successful yet little-known British innovations of the war, from which Hull would also eventually benefit.

Since 1937, Germany had been pushing to regain control of the city of Danzig (Gdansk), which had been ceded to Poland after the First World War. Fearing a German invasion, Poland formed an alliance with Great Britain and France, and the following month Hitler repudiated the German-Polish Non-Aggression Pact of 1934. The clock was ticking.

As tensions grew, on 22 August the painfully apt codeword 'Hastings' was transmitted to army units across the country, the first of a series that instructed units to move to a war footing. Royal Artillerymen converged on Wenlock Barracks, and two days later 173 and 266 Batteries dispersed to their predetermined positions around the city to set up their 3.7-inch anti-aircraft guns.[28] [29] Meanwhile, 286 Battery moved from Goole to Paull.[30]

On 31 August the SS faked a Polish border incursion as a pretext to invade. Even as the German army and Luftwaffe went into action the following day, the British government activated the pre-planned evacuation of children from larger towns and cities, and, as Haldane predicted, Hull was one of them. From 06:00 to 18:00, 50,000 youngsters – shepherded by their teachers and other guides – converged on the road, rail and ferry evacuation points for what for many was their first journey out of the city. Sixty-one trains departed both westwards and northwards from Paragon station alone, where a local journalist reported:

> It is now 08:30. Already more children have marched past me than I have seen in one company before. And I haven't seen a single tear! Even when the excursion leaves for a happy day at the seaside, you see harassed youngsters blubbering. But not here. We talked about it with an engine driver and a schoolmaster with a big yellow armlet marked 'Guide'. 'Most of 'em have been told it's a week's holiday,' said the Guide. 'Aye,' said the engine driver. 'A bloke says to me just now: "Hear them kids singing? They wouldn't be if they knew what it was about!" Don't be soft, I says. Do you want 'em to be roarin'?'
>
> It was the grown-ups who had lumps in their throats. 'I've never been nearer crying in my life,' said one of the railway officials, rustling his big pile of papers, 'than when the gates opened and the first lot came in. Such tiny tots… and one of 'em in sandshoes with his toes out.'

At the Corporation ferry pier:

> Seven o'clock and the haze on the river is lifting, promising sun after early rain that made the outlook black for officials as they rose on the most difficult day of the year. Men with red, yellow and white bands, women, too – and the first three schools are assembling for

departure into Lincolnshire. They are Marist College (average age 12), Southcoates-lane (average age 10), and Williamson-street (average age somewhere about seven)...

But many of these children from East Hull have never been on a boat before. When, at 7.45, they marched on to the *Wingfield Castle* and settled themselves on the lower and upper decks – the nippers from Williamson-street ranked as first-class passengers! – they were absorbed by river traffic. Breakfast was eaten with enormous gusto and a universal smell of orange. One small boy from Williamson-street insisted on sharing his bag of nuts with a pal.

'Our parents have been wonderful,' a head teacher said. 'We have instructed them carefully in all the procedure, but their response has been astonishing. Although it is a slum school, only four scholars turned up with inadequate food supply.'

Promptly at 8.30 a.m. the *Wingfield Castle* sailed into the sun for what one boy fondly called 'Lancashire'. Seven boats will sail through to-day, taking nearly 1,000 children to safer shores.[31]

On 3 September the UK declared war on Germany. Hull's first casualty of the conflict came just eight days later, when the submarine HMS *Oxley* was sunk in a friendly fire incident by the submarine HMS *Triton* off the coast of Norway, with the loss of most of her crew, including Hull Able Seaman Lawrence Stevenson.[32] The event was hushed up. Six days later five Hull men were killed when the aircraft carrier HMS *Courageous* was torpedoed by a German U-boat in the Western Approaches, the first naval loss of the war to enemy action.[33][34][35][36][37][38]

On 30 September the *Hull Daily Mail* reported on a decision that surely everybody had anticipated: the 1939 Hull Fair was cancelled, and all advance rents refunded.[39] The Walton Street fairground, though, was to make an honourable contribution to the war effort as a mooring point for barrage balloons, a tank training ground, and a car park for military vehicles.[40]

On 10 May 1940, German forces invaded France and the Low Countries. Four days later, as remnants of the Dutch army valiantly attempted to resist the German *Blitzkrieg*, the Luftwaffe fell upon the port of Rotterdam – which effectively had no anti-aircraft defences – killing 900 people, and destroying the medieval heart of the city. Militarily questionable, the raid was a stark lesson in how far aerial bombing had progressed since Madrid, Guernica, Barcelona, and even Warsaw.

In Britain, Rotterdam's fate was felt no more keenly than in Hull, as centuries of sea trade between the two great ports had forged strong bonds, as expressed by the *Hull Daily Mail*:

Hull folk feel particularly bitter about the invasion of Holland. We have had trade relations with the Low Countries for centuries, and, since the Dutch Wars, have fostered those on a basis which, for hundreds of Humberside folk, has become one of close personal friendship. We like the Dutch because they are so like ourselves.

The geographical situation of Rotterdam is almost identical with ours, and the people of Rotterdam have tackled their problems in a way which might serve as an example for Hull... The Dutch people have literally made their land – and have made it well. In construction of their 'polders' they have made miles of rich land from the very bed of the sea. It is shameful that all this decent, honest industry should be threatened.[41]

An unusual tragedy occurred at Wenlock Barracks on 19 May, when four soldiers of 286 Battery, Royal Artillery, were injured by the accidental discharge of a single rifle bullet. All four were admitted to the Hull Royal Infirmary, where one died eight days later. The subsequent inquest returned a verdict of accidental death.[42][43]

On the wider stage of the war, the remnants of the British Expeditionary Force had fallen back to Dunkirk. A number of Hull vessels took part in the evacuation – Operation Dynamo – between 26 May and 4 June, with four former trawlers from the port being sunk.[44]

# Chapter 3

# Overture: June 1940 to February 1941

On the night of 18/19 June 1940 the Luftwaffe began its concerted bombing campaign on Britain, aiming mostly for targets in the south-east of the country. Hull and the north-east were spared, but the city endured air-raid warnings lasting from midnight to dawn. The following night the attack shifted north in earnest.

The air-raid sirens sounded at 22:55 on the 19th, but it was not until after midnight that a cluster of approximately fifty-four IBs landed in east Hull, causing fires to twenty-nine domestic properties, but no casualties,[1] while a small number of 50kg High Explosive (HE) bombs resulted in a degree of minor infrastructure and railway damage (see Chapter 6). The all-clear sounded at 04:02.

Outside the city boundary, HEs and IBs landed in the vicinity of the Anglo-American Oil and Shell-Mex/British Petroleum (BP) facilities at Salt End, Hedon. With storage capacities of 24 million and 47 million gallons (109 million and 214 million litres), respectively, they were an obvious target, and the damage could have been colossal had the enemy attack been pressed home.[2] The area was protected by the barrage of 942 Balloon Squadron, which reported a total of eight HEs – two of which did not explode – and numerous IBs.[3]

The IBs pierced several tanks at the site, starting numerous fires. Shell-Mex/BP manager George Archibald Howe entered the compound and operated valves allowing the contents of breached tanks to be transferred to safe ones, assisted by Anglo-American manager William Sigsworth. Shell-Mex/ BP engineer George Samuel Sewell was at the forefront of the fire-fighting efforts, spraying foam whilst on the top of the burning tanks. Similar work was carried out by Fireman Jack Owen of the Hull Fire Brigade, despite his clothes being soaked in fuel in the process of reaching the top of one tank, while AFS Leading Fireman Clifford Turner took similar risks fixing hoses to the top of another burning tank. Shell-Mex/ BP handyman Thomas Gant assisted by tackling smaller blazes around the site. For their bravery, Howe, Sigsworth, Sewell, Owen and Turner were all awarded the George Medal, while Gant received an official Commendation.[4]

On the afternoon of the 20 June the *Hull Daily Mail* guardedly reported on the raids across the country, with what would become the standard pattern of the inflated claims of both sides, and a minimum of just about discernible local detail. Hull would almost never be named – even in the *Hull Daily Mail* – being instead euphemistically referred to as a 'North-East Coast Town', 'Northern Town', 'North Coast Town', or similar variations. This was not unique to Hull, and indeed the same vague descriptions were applied to a number of other places at the same time.

In an official communique the German authorities declared:

Last night air formations attacked with the heaviest bombs the important British armament centre of [ICI] Billingham [County Durham] with its nitrogen factories. Fierce fires, which

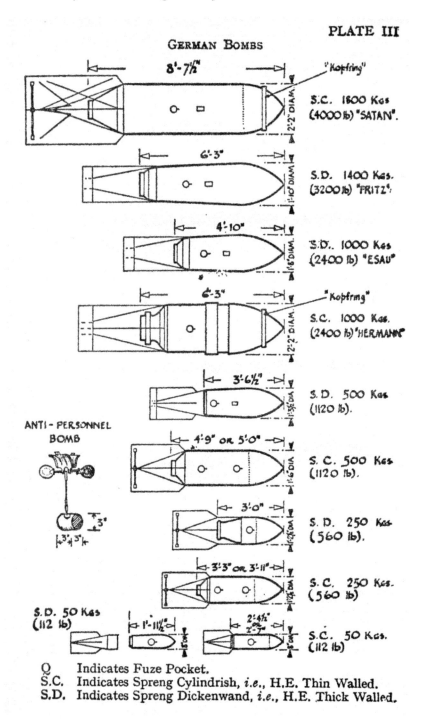

Schematic from a British 1941 bomb-disposal manual showing Luftwaffe ordnance, almost all of which were dropped on Hull at some point. Not shown are parachute mines or incendiary bombs, including the larger oil bombs.

were visible for 30 miles, showed the way to later attacking formations. Oil storage tanks in Hull were also set on fire.[5]

On the British side it was claimed that a number of enemy aircraft had been in action over the city, and that at least two of them were subsequently shot down over the Humber.[6] In fact, only one bomber came to grief in the region on the night, a Heinkel 111 that hit a barrage balloon at Billingham and crashed into the sea.[7]

Although Hull continued to endure nightly alerts after the first raid, no bombs were dropped on the city until almost a week later, when eleven 50kg HEs fell between Chamberlain Road and Lodge Street from 01:40 onwards on 26 June, causing slight property damage.[8] The area around King George Dock was also targeted with IBs, and there was some railway damage. There was one serious injury, but no deaths, and 942 Balloon Squadron reported at least two enemy aircraft down.[9]

The oil tanks at Salt End were less lucky on the night of 1/2 July, when a single Heinkel 111 attacked the facility after diverting from its primary target of the chemical works at Middlesbrough. The aircraft dropped sixteen 50kg HEs, setting one tank on fire, but suffered some anti-aircraft damage over Hull, before being shot up by three Spitfires of 616 Squadron from RAF Leconfield, and eventually ditching off Harwich. All four crew were picked up and taken prisoner by the sloop HMS *Black Swan*.[10]

At 05:15 on 11 July a single enemy aircraft was seen over Hull, but it beat a hasty retreat when anti-aircraft opened fire first (it dropped its bomb-load on a wreck at the mouth of the Humber as it departed).[11] Two 50kg HEs were dropped between Porter Street and Great Passage Street at 00:10 on 30 July, damaging flats.[12]

Thus far, apart from the first raid, damage had been purely residential, and it may have started to look like Hull was in for little more than sporadic and small-scale raiding. Instead the tempo changed in the early hours of 25 August, when eight 250kg HEs damaged properties in Carlton Street, Eastbourne Street, Rustenburg Street (when an Anderson Shelter was hit), and Morrill Street. Two people were killed in Carlton Street, and four in Rustenburg Street – the first fatalities in the city due to war operations (see Appendix 1) – and ten seriously injured. The raid could have been aimed at the power station in nearby Sculcoates Lane.[13] [14]

Around 21:40 on the following evening three clusters of IBs were dropped on Alexandra and Victoria Docks, and in the east of the city, but all were quickly extinguished before causing significant damage.[15] [16] At 02:31 on 28 August, seven or more 50kg HEs destroyed Hedon Road Maternity Home, and damaged Drypool Goods railway station on Seward Street.[17] [18] One injured man later died at Hull Royal Infirmary on Prospect Street, but there were no other serious casualties.

The Docks were again targeted around 02:20 on 30 August, when nine 50kg HEs and a single 250kg straddled Bellamy Street,[19] Williamson Street, and Victoria Dock.[20] That evening, a single Junkers 88 (out of a force of three that had set off to bomb the city) was caught by Hawker Hurricanes of 303 (Polish) Squadron to the east of Hull, and crash-landed near the village of Ottringham at 19:04. Two of the crew were injured, and taken to Hull Royal Infirmary for treatment, but died there.[21] The other two crewmen became prisoners of war.[22]

At 01:19 on 3 September seven HEs bombs landed in the Humber approximately 1 mile east of King George Dock.[23] [24] The next four raids were incendiary only, with attacks on 4, 6, 10 and 24 September. On each occasion the IBs were dealt with before much damage – if any – could be done.[25]

There was another HE-only raid at 20:20 on 13 October when four 50kgs straddled Stoneferry Road from Maxwell Street to Kathleen Road and Woodhall Street.[26] Returning from a walk, neighbours Marion Hairsine (22) and Doreen Walker (17) were caught in the blast of one bomb. Hairsine died immediately, and the injured Walker later the same day in hospital.[27]

At 01:42 on 22 October, Silverdale Road was hit by one of three 1,000kg Parachute Mines (PMs), the first to be dropped on the city, and the heaviest ordnance used by the Luftwaffe to date.[28] [29] [30] Primarily naval weapons, their descent was slowed by a parachute, and if landing in water they would arm themselves as magnetic mines. On land they operated as simple blast bombs, detonating on impact, or else initiating a timer and only exploding later. For reasons of inter-service demarcation, unexploded mines had to be defused by the Royal Navy rather than the army's Royal Engineers.

The morning of the first day of November saw up to a dozen 50kg HEs fall on Marfleet Avenue, Frodham Street and the railway beyond at 06:54. Eight people were seriously injured, with one – a fireman – dying in hospital three days later. Luftwaffe tactics then switched to early evening raids on 7, 8 and 11 November, with one cluster of IBs, then thirteen and five 50kg HEs, respectively, with the middle one causing a small number of serious injuries but no deaths.[31] [32] [33]

At 04:45 on 12 December an incendiary raid was scattered across Hedon Road, Bankside and Paragon Street, with most bombs put out. The last active raid of 1940 came on 17 December, when a single cluster of IBs was dropped on Greek Street and Woodlands Street, but no fires were started.[34] Across the country, raiding appeared to die down over Christmas, although it resumed on London in late December. The New Year, however, would be barely a week old when a tragedy far from Hull nevertheless impacted on the city.

The last most people in Hull had heard of Amy Johnson was in October 1939, when she was fined for her car headlights not complying with blackout regulations in Wales. In court,

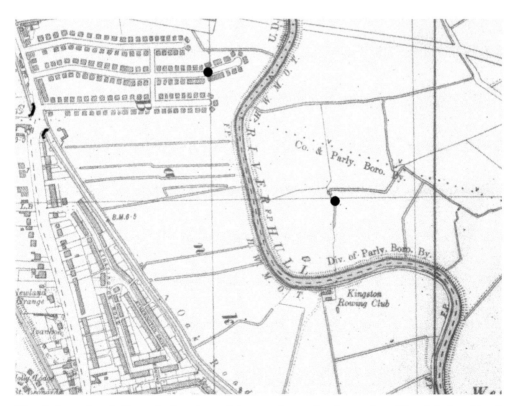

The circle markers indicate the locations of the parachute mine dropped on Silverdale Road (top) on 22 October, and another nearby.

An unexploded
parachute mine in an
east Hull garden.

the prosecuting barrister stated that after being arrested, and while being taken to the police station, 'she was very abusive and made use of language which, in my submission, is not becoming of a lady holding her position.' [35]

In May 1940, with little fanfare or publicity, Johnson joined the Air Transport Auxiliary, the civilian organisation that carried out aircraft ferrying duties for the services, and one of the few options for Britain's female pilots to use their skills and expertise in the air to aid the war effort. She had – with some reluctance – applied three months previously, and in the space on the application form which asked, 'Have you any foreign [flying] experience?' she drily wrote, 'Nearly all except S America.'[36]

On the night of 5 January 1941, while ferrying a twin-engined Airspeed Oxford trainer down from Scotland, Johnson bailed out over the Thames, having missed London and run out of fuel. Her parachute was spotted by the crew of HM trawler *Haslemere*, escorting a passing convoy, and Lt-Com. Walter Fletcher dived in to help her, but to no avail. Although he got back to his ship, he subsequently died of shock and exposure.

Much mystery surrounds Johnson's death, not least because some early reports stated that the *Haslemere* crew spotted two people in the water – a man and a woman – while other accounts said that she had been carrying an equally unidentified female passenger.[37] That she was carrying any passenger at all was quickly and officially denied. In recent years some have thought to embellish her fate with suggestions of a cover-up for propaganda purposes, suggesting 'friendly fire', or even that the *Haslemere* ran her over in the water, despite no compelling evidence of either.

In terms of air raids, the first five weeks of the year were quiet for Hull, broken at 23:10 on 4 February when a couple of 250kg HEs dropped on Goddard Avenue.[38] Four people were killed, with a fifth dying in hospital the following day. Although the sirens sounded at 17:28 on 11 February, no bombs were dropped, but a defective anti-aircraft shell that had not detonated at altitude proved the old adage, coming down to explode on Jalland Street. [39]

The Luftwaffe's Valentine's Day present to Hull was a bouquet of seven 50kg HEs, dropped at 19:00 either side of the River Hull, on Central Street and Glasshouse Row, damaging oil mills and warehouses.[40] This also marked a change of pace, as attacks subsequently became more frequent and/or heavier.

Luckily, although 16 February brought four 250kg HEs, they landed in fields around Hedon Road, but the evening of the 22nd saw a more varied bomb-load of two PMs, and single 250kg and 1,800kg HEs.[41] The latter was the largest type dropped on Hull, and was aptly nicknamed 'Satan' by the British military. The 250kg and the PMs (one unexploded)

Memorial to Amy Johnson in Prospect Street.
(Courtesy of Barnaby Cooper)

were scattered around Ellerby Grove and Rowlston Grove, causing extensive damage and four deaths. The 1,800kg HE with a delayed action fuse landed near the railway crossing at Hawthorn Grove, and exploded before it could be defused.

The night of 23/24 February saw four 250kg and two 500kg HEs, and at least three PMs across the city.[42] At 20:24, one bomb descended on the north end of De La Pole Avenue. The epicentre was two side terraces – Cleveland Avenue and Eva's Avenue. In his report the following day, Police Superintendent H. Jaram said:

> One very difficult rescue which was effected was when a woman [...] could be heard shouting and apparently injured. This was the last house at the end of the Avenue and debris was piled high against the parting wall. The foreman of the Rescue Party, James Kent at once squeezed his way between the debris, having to break pieces away, and he succeeded in getting down to the woman... She was trapped and Kent was handed a saw in order to get some of the debris away, but being in such a cramped position, this was a most difficult task. Kent received all the assistance that could be given and eventually the woman was rescued, but died. Foreman Kent, showing utter disregard for his own safety and risking serious injury to himself, climbed under the wreckage to effect the rescue of this woman and in my opinion his prompt action is deserving of very high praise and recognition.[43]

For his bravery 36-year-old Kent was awarded the George Medal.[44]

In all ten people died at the De La Pole Avenue site, and two more in hospital the same day. A thirteenth victim, Frederick Adamson, eventually died on 9 November 1946, the last known civilian death due to war operations in the city. Other streets hit that night were Hedon Road and Clough Road. The PMs ended up in Alexandra Dock, where two were detonated by sweeping operations.

On the night of 25/26 February, four IB clusters were scattered across north Hull, with two 250kg HEs on Kirby Street,[45] one of which was defused and removed by 4 March. At 12:02 on the 26th, an undetected PM – probably dropped two days previously – exploded in Alexandra Dock, sinking the lighters *Monarch* and *Brakelu*, and killing a dock worker.[46]

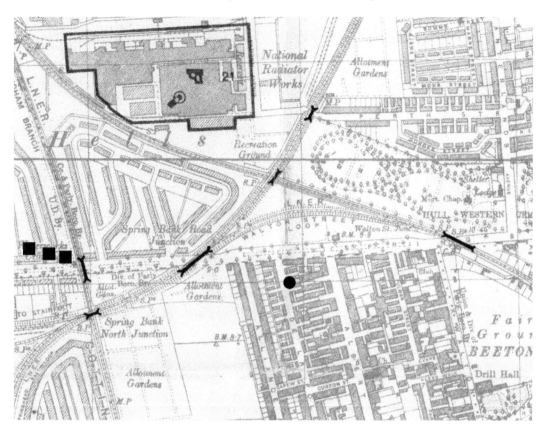

A landmine hit on De La Pole Avenue on 23 February 1941. The National Radiator Work to the north – accurately marked as a munitions factory – may have been the target. The square markers to the west indicate High Explosive bombs dropped during the same raid.

Haphazard post-war infill replaces the terraces destroyed on the east side of the north end of De La Pole Avenue.

# Chapter 4
# Crescendo: March to July 1941

The first night of March 1941 saw two PMs dropped at James Reckitt Avenue, killing five people and seriously injuring five more.[1] This brought the total death toll across the city to thirty-nine, over twenty-seven raids, in just under nine months. Some of the attacks were clearly targeting specific sites – or attempting to – or else may have been testing the city defences. Others were single lone aircraft, usually diverted from their primary targets, dropping their bomb-load on Hull on their way back to base. The next raid, on the night of 13/14 March, would be different.

The sirens sounded at 20:56, and the first bombs fell not long afterwards. At least 170 50kg HEs, and a pair each of 250kg and PMs, were dropped, with a total weight of 11 tons. The bombs were scattered widely across Stoneferry and north Hull, where Fifth Avenue School was hit, and there was widespread industrial and railway damage.[2] Forty people were either killed or later died from their injuries – more than all the previous raids put together. At least one of the attacking aircraft, a Dornier 17, was intercepted and shot down by a Bristol Beaufighter of 29 Squadron off Skegness, with the loss of all the crew.[3]

During the raid, AFS Assistant Commandant George Parker – who had already been on duty for 40 hours – was called to a fire at Meads Wharf, Lime Street, near North Bridge. Bombs were still falling, and Parker was blown some 30 yards (27m) by one explosion, which killed several other firemen. Despite this he stayed on duty, going on to supervise at a number of other fires; at one of these – at the East Yorkshire Motor Company's garage – he personally rescued a trapped man by ladder. He then returned briefly to the central fire station, before going to fetch the Revd Paley from Sutton, so that together they could break the sad news to the families of the dead firemen.[4]

At Sissons Brothers' paint works on Bankside, 33-year-old firewatcher Edward Saunders spotted an IB lodged in the roof of the varnish room at around 00:30. Climbing on top of the tanks, which contained highly inflammable varnish, he used an axe to get to the bomb, which he removed to a safe area. He then joined fellow firewatchers J. Broderick and H. Atkinson in fighting the fires around the premises until 07:00. For his actions he was awarded the British Empire Medal.[5][6]

The following night's raid was puny by comparison, with just single 50kg and 250kg HEs recorded, along with two PMs. One of the latter decimated De La Pole Terrace, on the west side of the north end of Bean Street, killing nineteen people.[7]

There was then a few days respite before the first official 'heavy' raid of the war, on the night of 18/19 March. Almost 250 HEs, mostly 50kg or 250kg, along with five PMs – just under 50 tons in all – saturated north and central Hull. Ninety-five people died, and more than sixty were seriously injured.[8]

Thirty-six-year-old Police War Reserve (PWR) Constable Francis William Ebbs was on duty patrolling a previously bombed laundry in Gladstone Street. At around 02:45, while in Wycliffe Grove, Argyle Street, a heavy bomb exploded about 10-12 yards (9-11m) from

The former National Cinema, which was bombed in March 1941. (Courtesy of Barnaby Cooper)

Another un-redeveloped bomb site: Nos 38–46, probably hit on 13–14 March 1941. (Courtesy of Barnaby Cooper)

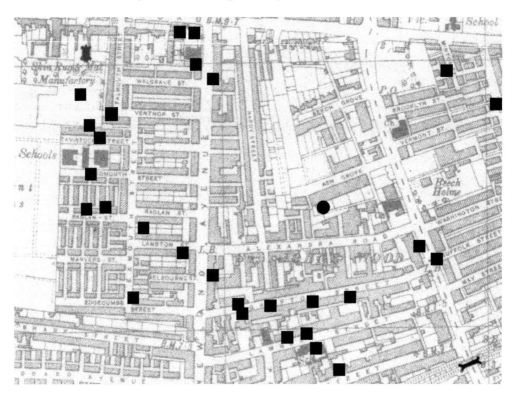

*Above*: Raglan Street (left-centre) was among many locations hit during the heavy raid of 13–14 March 1941.

*Left*: Lock-up garages have replaced the bombed houses on Raglan Street. (Courtesy of Barnaby Cooper)

him, demolishing an occupied air-raid shelter. Hearing the bomb fall, Ebbs threw himself to the ground, but was caught by the blast and covered in debris. Despite this, he went to assist those in the shelter and subsequently remained on duty until he was sent to the police station at 04:45, when the medical officer determined he was suffering from shock, and ordered him to go home.

Police Sergeant Thomas W. Sanderson reported:

> On arrival of the Rescue Party shortly afterwards he asked to be allowed to take the party to the people trapped in the shelter and as I realised that time would be saved I told him to do so. He continued to assist the rescue parties as they arrived and made no further complaint to me of his condition and continued to work with the rescue parties until 4.40 a.m. when he reported to me at the incident post... Throughout the time Ebbs worked at this incident he never asked to be relived on account of his condition and had I realised that he was badly shocked as has since been revealed, I should have ordered him to a First Aid Post for treatment.[9]

March closed with two 50kg HEs and twelve PMs (two unexploded) across Ferensway, Freehold Street, Boulevard, Hedon Road, Prospect Street (hitting the Royal Infirmary), and Priory Sidings.[10] There was extensive railway and industrial damage, and forty-four people died – thirteen alone at a shelter on Ferensway – and more than seventy seriously injured.[11]

The ARP Control Centre on the corner of Ferensway and Spring Bank was hit, and 42-year-old Dr David Diamond, the city's Deputy Medical Officer of Health, was killed, along with 46-year-old Constable Robert Garton, who was on duty outside.[12] A number

House on East Hull Estate collapsed by a high-explosive bomb on 31 March–1 April.

The post-war replacement blends in well (reverse angle). (Courtesy of Barnaby Cooper)

The ARP control on Ferensway, which was gutted on 31 March 1941.

of people were injured, and fire took hold of the building. Councillor Leonard Speight, the Controller and Chairman of Emergency Committee, co-ordinated the transfer of the Control to an alternate location, where he remained on duty for the duration of the raid. For these actions he was made an Officer of the Order of the British Empire (OBE).[13]

The death toll amongst those in the air-raid shelter on Ferensway set an unfortunate precedent. Although many households in the outer parts of the city could rely on the ubiquitous and surprisingly resilient Anderson Shelter, many Hull families still lived in crowded terraces with no gardens. The only solution for them was communal street shelters, which consisted of a thick concrete slab roof supported by brick walls.

Unfortunately, although these provided good protection from splinters and shrapnel, even near misses had a nasty tendency to blow out the shelter walls, causing the often intact roof to pancake onto the rubble, and anyone who happened to be in the shelter at the time. Many people were killed when this happened, although equally the rescue squads quickly devised a way of lifting up the roof slab, which became known as the 'Hull Lift Method'.[14]

On 3 April there was an incendiary raid on east Hull, with most of them being put out and little damage, although a firewatcher was injured and later died.[15] Just after midnight on 7/8 April, a single 250kg HE was dropped on Spring Bank West, along with a 1,000kg bomb that did not explode until the following afternoon.[16] There then followed an incendiary-only raid on 9/10 April, with four clusters dropped across south-east and central Hull.[17]

For the next raid, on the night of 15/16 April, three clusters of IBs were augmented by six PMs (one unexploded). These fell mainly on east Hull, between Holderness Road and Hedon Road, and as far south as Alexandra Dock.[18] At the east end of Holderness Road, one of the PMs obliterated Ellis Terrace,[19] killing twenty-six people there, one person in neighbouring Bright Street, and fourteen in Studley Street. The latter included perhaps Hull's youngest war casualty, a baby girl born in situ only a few hours previously.[20] To the east, another shelter was hit in Hotham Street, killing five people, along with two more in the street, and injuring a third. In all, fifty-seven people died as a result of the raid, and twenty more were seriously injured.

No bombs fell during the next ten days, although two defective anti-aircraft shells fired during an alert on 23/24 April destroyed houses in St George's Road and Glasgow Street.[21] On

The Presbyterian church
on Prospect Street,
which was gutted on
31 March–1 April.

Now replaced by the
Central Library. (Courtesy
of Barnaby Cooper)

the night of 25/26 April two clusters of IBs were dropped, along with a pair of PMs. One of the latter landed at the corner of Council Avenue and Lakeside Grove in Gipsyville, killing eight people and seriously injuring four more. The following night two more PMs were dropped in fields near Kingston High School, causing slight residential damage to nearby Lynton Avenue.[22]

There was another lull for a week, before a minor raid on the night of 3/4 May. A single PM was dropped on Alexandra Dock, and the first G-Mine (GM – *bomenmine* in German) on the premises of J.H. Fenner & Company on Marfleet Avenue.[23] The G-Mine was a modified naval mine designed for use against land targets, with Bakelite fins instead of a parachute. Two nights later a single 250kg HE was dropped on King George Dock.[24]

The next heavy raid came on the night of 7/8 May. In terms of overall tonnage it was actually slightly smaller than the raid of 18/19 March, but the composition ensured more than double the fatalities. A hundred assorted HEs, and a staggering twenty-eight PMs or GMs weighing some 45 tons were dropped, along with ten clusters of IBs.[25] Added to the conflagration was a single Oil Bomb (OB) – or *flammenbombe* in German – the first to be dropped on the city.[26] These were 250kg or 500kg bomb casings filled with a liquid incendiary mixture of 30 per cent benzene and 70 per cent petrol, with a TNT bursting charge, which often failed.[27][28]

The eastern and western docks were the main focus of the attack, as well as industrial targets along the banks of the Hull, but the city's main retail district along King Edward

Prospect Street decimated after the 31 March–1 April raid.

A very different modern view.
(Courtesy of Barnaby Cooper)

Street, Jameson Street, and Prospect Street were largely destroyed. In Victoria Square the landmark Prudential Tower on the insurance company's offices was left an empty shell. Many people had been sheltering in the building basement, and fifteen were killed there.

At 01:19, 942 Balloon Squadron's A Flight's headquarters at 4 Hamlyn Avenue, Anlaby Road, were gutted by fire, and other Flights reported numerous fires, HEs and PMs in their immediate vicinity. A direct hit on the Island Pier[29] killed one airman of the Squadron,[30] and injured four others.[31]

The military losses, however, were not all one-sided. Three Heinkel 111s were engaged by a Hurricane of 151 Squadron from RAF Wittering, two successfully, with one ditching off Withernsea. Two of the crew were rescued and taken prisoner, but the other two could not be recovered and so died.[32] One body washed up at Holmpton later the same day, and was buried in St Mary's churchyard in Brandesburton alongside another Luftwaffe airman, who had been killed whilst on a coastal reconnaissance mission eight days previously (see Appendix 2).

Story Street
after the raid of
31 March–1 April 1941.

Not much has changed
here, except the type
of shops. (Courtesy of
Barnaby Cooper)

While on duty fire-watching at a branch of the Employment Exchange on Albion Street where he was a temporary clerk, 40-year-old ex-trawlerman Henry 'Harry' Lamb assisted AFS personnel in tackling a fire spreading from an adjacent congregational church, for which he received the British Empire Medal.[33][34]

Near to Paragon station, Osborne Street was hit by a PM on the corner of Myton Street. Three people were killed at the Osborne Street Shelter, and numerous buildings demolished. The Myton Arms public house was flattened, trapping the manager, 39-year-old Arthur John Pizzey, and his wife in the cellar where they had been sheltering. As the cellar began to fill with water, Pizzey attempted to find a way out, while his wife blew a whistle to try to attract attention. After an hour or so the whistling was heard by 18-year-old firewatcher Gerald Shakespeare, who shouted down to them. Mr Pizzey later recounted:

> We told him [who we were] and he said 'You'll have to hang on till I get some help,' and then he went away. At this time there was about 4 feet of water in the cellar and my wife and I had mounted a gantry and boxes to escape it. We had to crouch down with our heads touching the ceiling.[35]

The landmark Prudential Tower in Victoria Square before the war.

The same location after the raid on 7–8 May 1941.

After a few minutes, Shakespeare returned with fellow firewatcher Fred Foster (also 18). Pizzey continued:

> I heard them commence to clear debris from the Osborne Street side of the cellar in spite of the fact that terrific enemy action was progressing. Eventually they succeeded in clearing a space of about 2 feet square through which I pushed my wife, and I followed her.
>
> At this time the water in the cellar had risen to about 4 feet 6 inches, leaving only 18 inches of air space between its surface and the ceiling of the cellar. When I reached the street I found that the debris above the cellar was alight and that the roads were flooding with water apparently from a large water main.
>
> The two youths, Shakespeare and Foster, treated the matter quite casually, refusing to disclose their identity and remarking that someone else may be needing their assistance while they were talking to me. After conducting me by the safest road towards the Paragon Station Hotel, they went away.[36]

Prior to this rescue Shakespeare and Foster had already tackled an IB in a building next door to the one they were watching on South Street (that of their employers, Gilberts Ltd), and afterwards warned the driver of a passing AFS truck that the rear cover of the vehicle was on fire, which they helped to put out. After leaving the Pizzeys, they went on to assist in salvaging goods at the bombed premises of Wm Jackson & Sons on Paragon Street until 04:30, after which they returned to their employer's premises to salvage goods there.[37] Despite their efforts to avoid 'publicity', both youths received official commendations. [38]

At Princes Dock, a fire-float[39] crewed by 41-year-old Leading Fireman Tom Bulliver Fowler, 45-year-old Firemen Harold Barker, and 40-year-old Stanley Simpson of the AFS continued to pump water to the fire-fighting teams at work on the dockside and as far as Victoria Square, making up for the loss of supply due to fractured mains. Divisional Fire Officer W.M. Finlayson stated that the men carried on, despite being affected by fumes coming from the fire-float engine's broken manifold, and that 'Although it was not their precise work, these men assisted to run lengths of hose from the fire float into King Edward Street at which point the fires were burning most fiercely.'[40]

Just north of Victoria Dock, a PM demolished some twenty houses at the south end of Naylors Row, near the junction with Thomas Street,[41] killing ten people and trapping others. Recovery operations were led by 50-year-old rescue party foreman John Christopher Staveley, a task hampered by the fact that with so many blazes across the city, no fire service personnel could attend to those in the immediate vicinity. It was later reported:

> Foreman Staveley continued to direct rescue operations up to and beyond the scene of the fires, by allocating certain men to the control of the fires, whilst at the same time arranging reliefs for rescuers as they reached the limits of their endurance. At the same time, the foreman displayed great coolness and knowledge of organisation by arranging for all rescued persons to be carried to a small house in the vicinity which he used as a casualty clearing centre and his temporary headquarters until the arrival of a first aid party. In this way 12 persons were made comfortable after rescue operations and handed over to the First Aid Services, and the bodies of 6 persons were recovered.[42]

William Wright Dock was extensively hit by HEs, IBs and PMs. Fifty-year-old Hull City Police Constable Thomas Henry Furniss organised an ad hoc fire-fighting unit comprising

Grain and debris from Rank's flour mill slides into the River Hull after the 7–8 May 1941 raid.

himself and 49-year-old LNER Police Constable (Temporary) George Edward Scott, along with 32-year-old John Williams and 39-year-old Alfred Richard Scott, Petty Officer Cook and Steward, respectively, in the Royal Navy. It was later reported that after IBs and HEs started and spread numerous fires around the dockside warehouses and railway wagons:

> Two Parachute Mines were dropped, one exploding in Goulton Street, near Exchange Sidings, overturning some ten to fifteen wagons and extensively damaging others. The other mine fell in the sidings, tearing up railway metals, overturning wagons and damaging several others. There would be in the sidings at that time about 300 wagons containing wheat, timber and coal.
>
> From when the wagons were first set alight, and for about two hours, the [...] men continued to attack the burning wagons, putting out the fires in all of them except three, which they isolated by uncoupling them and... pushing them away by hand.
>
> Practically all the time they were working in the siding a large amount of heavy debris was thrown all over and in fact one H.E. bomb had dropped on a steel lighter in the Dry Dock... which threw a very large piece on to No. 29 Shed and other pieces on the railway sidings. Regardless of this danger, and danger from other H.E. bombs, these men by their courage, initiative and perseverance were responsible for saving numerous wagons and valuable foodstuffs.[43]

All four men were recommended for an official commendation, but in the end all bar George Edward Scott received one.[44] [45]

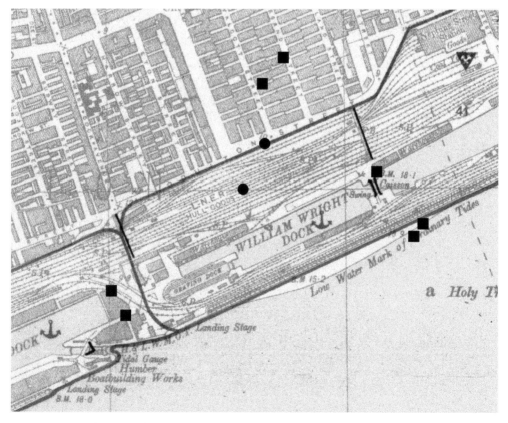

Hits around William Wright Dock on 7–8 May 1941.

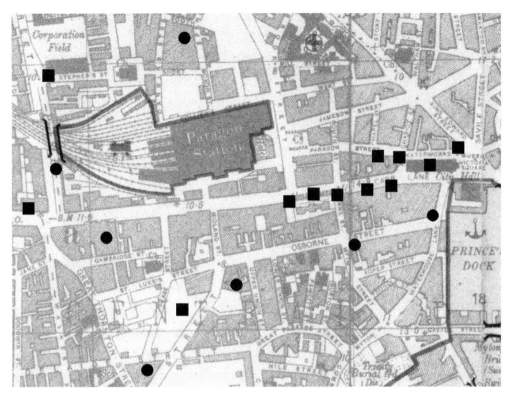

The area around Paragon station during both of the May 1941 heavy raids.

At the adjacent St Andrew's Dock, 52-year-old William Summers was working on No. 3 Oil Boat when an explosion on the dockside threw him into the engine room and a shipmate overboard into the water. Despite his own injuries (included a fractured rib), and after several attempts, Summers succeeded in pulling his comrade back on board, before taking him ashore for medical attention.[46] He also received an official commendation.[47]

Near Railway Dock, a single OB landed on the roof of the straw loft of the LNER stables on the north side of Lister Street. Sixty-year-old Stable Foreman and Great War veteran George Hinch were instrumental in leading thirty-three horses to safety, although four perished in the fire. For his leadership, initiative and courage, Hinch was awarded the British Empire Medal.[48][49]

One of the most tragic incidents occurred at Lister Street, where a number of houses were demolished around 01:45, with numerous people killed or trapped. Initially acting alone, 32-year-old Harry Gelder Cardwell tunnelled his way from an adjoining property towards the basement kitchen of no. 37, where members of the Dove family were still alive, although the debris of the house was on fire. He made contact with 15-year-old Beatrice Dove, but an explosion at 03:00 caused much shifting of rubble, and the other members of her family fell silent. Cardwell stayed with the girl, making several attempts to provide her water, which proved impossible in the cramped confines of the tunnel. Returning to the surface at around 11:30, he found that 16-year-old AFS messenger James Alfred Hodgson was prepared to try. Hodgson later recounted:

> Cardwell assisted me through the debris which was still crumbling and hot, and with great difficulty I forced my way close up to the girl and found she was lying on a couch with just her face and one hand showing.

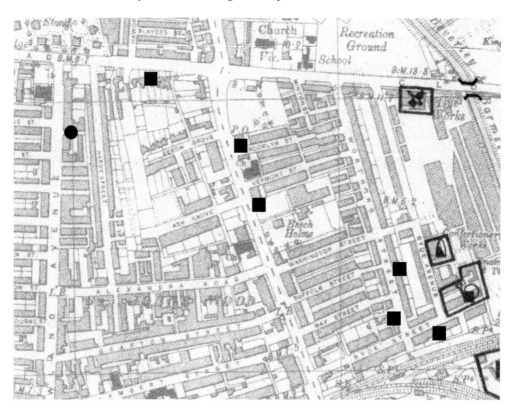

*Above*: High-explosive bomb and landmine hits around Newland Avenue during the heavy raids of May 1941.

*Left*: A post-war infill at the northern end of Newland Avenue. (Courtesy of Barnaby Cooper)

I stayed alongside her for fifteen minutes, talking about the pictures, and she was quite conscious and asked for a drink. I got a medicine bottle full of water and attempted to give her a drink from this, but owing to the cramped nature of the place, I was unable to tip the bottle up sufficient to get water into her mouth. I asked for a child's feeding bottle, which was filled with water, and by using this I was able to give her the drink she had requested.

She was complaining of being hot, so I got a stirrup pump which was operated by Cardwell, and I was able to damp all the debris round her and cool her face with the water. All this time the Rescue Squad were working on the removal of the material which was trapping the girl, and bricks and mortar were falling all around me and the girl, so I put protection over her face to keep the stuff from falling on her.[50]

Hodgson then returned to the surface, but before Cardwell could go back down the tunnel, the debris of the house shifted again, and Beatrice was killed. This was around 12:30, and Cardwell stayed on the scene until all the bodies had been recovered by 19:00.[51] He was subsequently awarded the George Medal, and Hodgson the British Empire Medal. [52]

On the same night a George Medal was earned by LNER Wagon Examiner Fred Potter for tackling a fire unaided, and saving horses from a burning stable.[53] Inspector Thomas Henry Rumsey of the Hull Police Fire Brigade was awarded the British Empire Medal for leading fire-fighting efforts at Paragon station.[54][55]

For much of the rest of the 8th of May the people of Hull did the best they could to pick up the pieces of the raid. Rescue efforts carried on into the afternoon and early evening, while the debris-strewn streets were cleared. Too dangerous to be left standing, the Prudential Tower was unceremoniously dynamited. At the Hull Corporation Telephone Department on Anlaby Road,[56] a team of six GPO engineers from York endeavoured to restore the trunk lines out of the city until late into the evening.

The view to the Town Hall along Waterhouse Lane, obliterated by a landmine during the May 1941 heavy raids.

Now blocked after the building of the Prince's Quay shopping centre. (Courtesy of Barnaby Cooper)

Just after midnight the Luftwaffe returned for what they must have thought would surely be the knockout blow. The number of bombs dropped on the city was around two-thirds higher than the previous night: almost 200 HEs, over forty PMs or GMs (weighing 76 tons), along with twelve IB clusters and two OBs.[57] [58] This was the heaviest raid on the city of the war.

As had happened previously, the main bomber force was augmented by aircraft from other formations, which either failed to find their primary targets or else were re-routed under orders before they reached them. The pathfinder unit *Kampfgruppe 100* set off to mark Derby with flares, but could not locate the city due to British jamming of the German *X-Gerät* navigational radio beam. The aircraft of the formation then tried to find alternative targets, and while some chose Nottingham, four joined the existing heavy assault on Hull.[59] One Heinkel 111 heading for Sheffield was diverted to join the assault on Hull, but was intercepted by a Boulton Paul Defiant night-fighter and shot down over Long Riston, near Beverley. Two of the crew were taken prisoner, but the other two died.[60]

Over Hull itself a Hawker Hurricane of 255 Squadron from RAF Kirton-in-Lindsey engaged two Heinkel 111s, one of which was seen to fall into the Humber, with the loss of its five-man crew.[61] Two Heinkels targeting Sheffield came to grief in East Yorkshire, one being shot down at Sunk Island, the other near Patrington. One crew member from each survived to be taken prisoner, but the other eight were killed, with seven of them being subsequently buried in St Mary's churchyard in Brandesburton[62] (see Appendix 2).

The bomb-damaged Guildhall.

The post-war repair has weathered well. (Courtesy of Barnaby Cooper)

At the start of the raid, north-east of Alexandra Dock, a stick of three HEs straddled the north end of Woodhouse and Wyke Streets, with one of the latter's communal shelters being demolished. Almost immediately, five members of the Parsons family were rescued by Bert Sensier, Percy William Cannon and his 18-year-old son James Bernard Cannon, who managed to remove a section of the shelter roof above the family.

Before long 43-year-old Police Inspector Albert Edward Evans arrived on the scene and took charge. Along with 26-year-old Police Constable John Charles Dickinson and 30-year-old bus conductor Stanley Mainprize, he succeeded in rescuing a number of people trapped under the shelter debris, although three of the occupants had been killed. One woman, although alive, was trapped by the leg between the remains of a bunk and part of the shelter roof, so had to wait for the arrival of the rescue party several hours later. In the meantime, Evans was assisted by 32-year-old Casualty Service member Lawrence Giblin, who crawled into the shelter debris to administer first aid.[63] Evans was awarded the British Empire Medal, while Dickinson, Giblin and Mainprize received official commendations.[64][65]

With the area around the docks and the River Hull waterfront being targeted, the historic High Street was hit in numerous places. At 00:25 a heavy pump arrived, driven by 30-year-old John Coletta,[66] but had to be sent away due to the lack of available water.

Damage to the north side of the General Post Office in Alfred Gelder Street.

Another flawless repair job. (Courtesy of Barnaby Cooper)

Coletta, however, volunteered to remain, and he was given charge of a hose in front of the Wilberforce House Museum, which he played on an adjoining blazing warehouse, even when it began to collapse. In charge of the operation, Leading Fireman Wilfred Charles Clarke later recounted:

> This action, in itself, was beyond praise, but later in the raid, I found it necessary to run a further line of hose through the Museum to the warehouse laying between it and the river. It was then necessary for a hose to be played on the back wall of the Museum, which was separated by a distance of only six feet from the wall of the blazing five storey warehouse.
>
> Coletta insisted on staying in the narrow alley so formed, although the five storey wall was expected to fall at any moment. In this place the heat was terrific, but Coletta repeatedly declined to hand over his branch to a relief...
>
> Coletta had been working continuously under great danger during the 'blitz' of the previous night and must have been fatigued. Incidentally, he was suffering from blast in the eyes.
>
> His courage was an inspiration and help to me and all our colleagues. We are proud to do service with him.[67]

This account was corroborated by Air Raid Warden Lawrence Eric Lockwood, who stated, 'I have no doubt that Wilberforce House was saved as a result of this fireman's exertions and carrying on with complete disregard for his own safety.'[68]

Coletta was awarded the George Medal for his actions, but for which one of Hull's most historic buildings may well have been lost.[69] He subsequently donated his medal to Wilberforce House, where it remains to this day.[70]

Late on the evening of the 8th, 17-year-old ARP Cyclist Messenger Donald Noble had rescued a woman and three children from the debris of their house in the Drypool area, and led them to a welfare centre. He then returned to assist in digging out the woman's husband and four more children. After the start of the new raid, he was helping Warden W. Ledger and Police Constable Leon Tansley extinguish IBs in a garage when an HE exploded nearby. Tansley was left temporarily blinded and disorientated, so Noble and Ledger took him to a First Aid Post (FAP). Not long afterwards, the Warden's son, 31-year-old James Ashton Ledger, was injured at Church Street. It was later reported:

> ... as all lines of communication were out of action, Messenger Noble was contacted and went to Malton Street School First Aid Post through a hail of fire and shell splinters. The school was on fire and no service was available. Using a shutter for a stretcher, Mr Ledger's son was taken to a shelter to which a doctor was called. Noble and another man took the injured man to [another] First Aid Post by lorry, but unfortunately he died the same day.[71]

Noble received an official commendation.[72] He was one of around 2,000 volunteer civil defence messengers who served in Hull during the war. All were cyclists aged 15 and over, both male and female. They proved invaluable in conveying vital messages when telephone lines are cut and roads too blocked with debris to allow motor vehicle access. If routes were impassable even to the messengers' bicycles, they would continue on foot, with or without their machine on their back.[73] Three of them were killed during air raids – a 17-year-old girl and two 18-year-old boys.

At New George Street the premises of oil merchant Thelwalls was set on fire, sending blazing oil flowing down the street. Just after 02:00, 34-year-old Leading Fireman Arthur Bucknall and 41-year-old Auxiliary Fireman Tom Davison were sent to attend with a light pump towed by the car of 52-year-old civilian volunteer driver George Edward Blades. AFS Patrol Officer William Gill stated that the three men:

The imposing premises of WHSmith in Jameson Street, gutted by fire.

The post-war rebuild, with minimal decoration, save for the city shield at the apex. (Courtesy of Barnaby Cooper)

...were engaged continually on this fire and about 3 a.m. I actually visited these three men who were busily engaged in pumping water from the sewers on to the fire at Messers Thelwalls. The premises were well alight and at that particular time enemy aircraft were apparently using this fire as a target.

These three men continued in their work despite the bombing and they were the only men engaged on the New George Street fire.

Later the same day I ascertained from Bucknall, Davison and Blades that they were the men responsible for saving a woman and [her] children from fire at a house in New George Street.[74]

The woman in question, Elizabeth Teece, said that when the raid started, she sent her eldest son Jack and two of her youngest children, 9-year-old Ethel and 2-year-old Campbell, to her husband's works shelter, but before she could follow with the other three children, they were trapped by the fire:

I tried the front door, but when I opened it the flames rushed into the house. I shouted for help but no one seemed to hear me and I was quickly becoming exhausted. I then attracted

The southern end of High Street after the attack on 9 May 1941.

Virtually unrecognisable today. (Courtesy of Barnaby Cooper)

the attention of someone because I heard him say, 'Good God, there is a woman and some kids in there.'

A few minutes later two firemen rushed into the house through the front door and by that time the flames were as high as the house and the heat was unbearable. One took hold of Dorothy [16], who was then in a collapsed condition, put something over her head, and dashed out of the house with her. The other fireman carried Alfred [11] out to safety. A few minutes later another fireman came through the flames into the house and put a blanket over the baby's head and guided me through the flames into the street. The baby Brian [5 months] sustained a severe burn to his left eye and head.

I am satisfied that unless those firemen had come to our assistance I should have collapsed and no doubt my children would have suffered the same fate, and I should like to mention at this stage how thankful I am to those three heroes.[75]

All three men were awarded the British Empire Medal.[76]

When the raid began, the GPO engineers at the Telephone Department had taken shelter in vaults below the nearby Trinity Almshouses. At around 02:40 a stick of HEs straddled the Telephone Department building and the Almshouses, destroying the latter, killing two residents, and trapping others in the wreckage, which collapsed into the vaults below. The rescue efforts were carried out by parties led by 52-year-old foremen Harry Moore and 35-year-old George Walker, who both received official commendations,[77] [78] as did 44-year-old Police Constables Herbert Henry Cheeseman and 38-year-old Charles William Ward, who were instrumental in releasing the trapped telephone engineers.[79] [80]

The area around Nornabell Street was particularly badly hit. In Barnsley Street an HE demolished four houses and damaged several more, and Sergeant Harry Jarvis and Constable Stanley Rowland Flick of the City Police were instrumental in rescuing John Wright of 11 Thomas Terrace. Using a hammer and chisel, they broke through a collapsed wall, roof rafters and a ceiling to find – after some two hours – Wright wrapped in the remains of his mattress and bedding, which had undoubtedly saved him.[81] In the same area, 50-year-old civilian Daniel Baines was active in rescuing trapped neighbours and assisting in fire-fighting efforts, for which he received an official commendation.[82] [83]

The nearest FAP to Nornabell Street was at the East Hull Clinic at Morrill Street,[84] where 53-year-old Dr Leslie Frederick Wilson was in charge. Wilson had trained and organised his staff rigorously and efficiently from when the FAP was first established, which paid off

Close proximity to Paragon station resulted in the destruction of the Trinity Almshouse on 9 May 1941.

The utilitarian replacement buildings included the new Cecil Cinema on the far right. Kingston Communications, successor to the Corporation Telephone Department, still occupies the site on the left. One of the K6 telephone kiosks is the traditional Hull white, and the other colours of Hull City FC. (Courtesy of Barnaby Cooper)

during both this and the previous raid, as each night over 100 casualties passed through the Post.[85] He later recalled:

> A blockage of the road prevented any ambulances getting to us so the staff improvised a temporary hospital at the first-aid post. There we worked with only the aid of hurricane lights and candles. We had stoves, too, to heat the premises, and we had to stop the use of water brought for any purpose other than which was absolutely necessary.[86]

On this second night, due to the chaos in the surrounding streets, forty-five patients had to be retained at the FAP overnight, as they could not be transported to hospital, and all survived their extended stay.[87]

At Abbey Street an Oil Bomb started a large fire in an adjoining property, which threatened Horsley, Smith & Company. With insufficient mains water pressure, 25-year-old Police Constable Walter Harry Dixon, aided by some firewatchers, had to try to soak stores of timber using stirrup pumps. He then supervised the evacuation of 40–50 occupants from the firm's air-raid shelter, as well as others from shelters in Bellamy Street, which were in danger from a fire at White's Sugar Mill in Williamson Street.[88] Dixon then rendered first aid to one of the firewatchers, before supervising the removal of a number of vehicles threatened by the fire. As these had been immobilised (as an anti-invasion precaution), one employee used the firm's electric truck to tow them away.[89]

A PM landed at the junction of Liberty Lane and Market Place, setting fire to the premises of Goddard, Walker and Brown Ltd. Arriving on the scene, the rescue party led by 47-year-old Foreman William Irwin was told by an ARP Warden that the premises were well alight, and nothing could be done. Ignoring this, Irwin investigated, finding a rapidly spreading fire and a demolished works shelter covered with burning debris, yet with survivors still alive.

> Hearing cries for help at the point the fire had reached, the foreman found a man badly trapped and unconscious. After strenuous efforts, this man and two others were rescued alive and removed. The heat was so intense and the fire so close that the clothes of the trapped persons were constantly catching fire and the members of the rescue party were burned about the hands through handling hot debris. Fire eventually forced the party back as they continued to search, without success. During the whole of the operations bombs of many kind were exploding around the rescue party, which was ringed by fire, but they worked until no further rescue work could be done because of fires.[90]

For his determination and leadership, Irwin was awarded the British Empire Medal.[91]

Sergeant Harold Marriott (40) of the Hull City Police Fire Brigade's Hedon Road Divisional Station came in for praise for exceptional leadership and initiative during both raids. Superintendent T.H. Barker stated:

> Having got the fires at his Station under control, a very heavy calibre bomb fell several feet away from the Control Room, extinguished the lights, broke all communications and again set the building on fire. Marriott, after fighting huge fires all night, refused to rest and went in search of another building to use as a Station. A building having been secured, he superintended the removal of equipment and when this was done, got to work on his appliance to make ready for further raids. The following day Marriott was still working at full pressure and I had to order him to cease and rest for a short period. His conduct was such that it inspired all who came in contact with him and his men were inspired by his leadership and determination.[92]

Marriott was also awarded the British Empire Medal.[93]

Further north on High Street, after the raid.

More peaceful now. Most of the damaged buildings have been replaced, but some originals survive. (Courtesy of Barnaby Cooper)

Outside the city boundary, IBs again fell on the oil depot at Salt End, with two landing on the roof of a large tank, and burning through. The vapour inside ignited as fierce jets of flame, marking the target for the bombers. Shell-Mex/BP manager George Samuel Sewell GM climbed to the top of the tank, and sandbagged the holes, extinguishing the fires. He then climbed another tank in order to kick a third IB from it. For these acts he was awarded a bar to the George Medal he earned on 20 June 1940.[94]

After two consecutive nights of such devastation, the people of Hull faced the evening of 9 May with dread expectation. Parts of the city were still burning, making it easy to find if the Luftwaffe were determined to finish the job. The sirens sounded at 23:40, but all that came was a single aircraft, which dropped its four HEs on fields just north of the junction of Sutton Road and Leads Road at 01:20. Another small raid came in the early hours of 12 May, causing a small amount of residential damage. Over a fortnight later there was another attack on the night of 28/29 May, resulting in limited railway damage.[95]

Extensive damage to Humber Street after the 9 May 1941 raid.

Little rebuilding here. (Courtesy of Barnaby Cooper)

An alert late on the evening of 2 June seemed to have passed off peacefully when the all-clear sounded at 23:55, but seven minutes later a pair of 50kg and 250kgs HEs were dropped.[96] They fell in a line from Margaret Street, through Park Grove/Princes Avenue and Blenheim Street, to Marlborough Avenue, killing four, six, fifteen and four people, respectively – twenty-eight in all.

At No. 50 Blenheim Street, tunnelling operations by a rescue party continued for more than seven hours to try to save nine members of the Elston/Denton family, but only one person – an 11-year-old girl – was found alive. In charge of the rescue party, E. Mars reported:

> It was found impossible to release the child without further work from the top of the debris, so a shaft was sunk and after a further 2½ hours the child was extricated, apparently little the worse. She had been conscious during the whole of this period and had been able to assist the rescue operation by directing the party in their work.

Market Place, which was damaged on 9 May 1941.

Damage to riverside warehouses.

Throughout the whole of the above rescue, volunteer [Enoch Emmerson] Jacklin's efforts had been untiring and he was the leading hand in the tunnelling and shafting operations. In spite of the considerable period which the operations covered, Jacklin insisted on carrying on with the job until the child was released, and he was undoubtedly responsible for the saving of her life.[97]

There were three more raids in June – on the 10th, 23rd and 29th – with only the last being substantial. Even so, the fifty 50kg HEs and five clusters of IBs dropped caused mainly domestic damage,[98] with just one HE hitting the King George Dock. Five people were seriously injured, and one killed – Assistant Chief Constable James Smith of the City Police. He was the most senior of six police officers killed during air raids in the city.[99]

On 11 July fifty-five HEs and a single PM weighing about 13 tons in all – along with six IB clusters – killed twenty-two civilians and one Merchant Seaman, and seriously injured a further forty-six, mainly in and around Fenchurch Street. On the western outskirts of the city, two HEs hit Francis Askew School[100] and a nearby railway embankment. The school

Mason Street after the attack on 23–24 June 1941.

The Hull History Centre on the site of Mason Street. (Courtesy of Barnaby Cooper)

contained an FAP, where a large number of civil defence personnel were gathered at the time. Six people were killed, while a seventh died of his injuries nineteen months later.

Shortly after one particular Heinkel 111 had dropped its bombs, it was repeatedly engaged by a British fighter (possibly a Defiant of 255 Squadron), and the pilot ditched the bomber off Flamborough Head. One of the crew drowned, while the other three were picked up by a minesweeper and taken prisoner.[101]

On 15 July there was another medium-sized raid on Hull, with twenty-five HEs and five GMs dropped on North Hull Estate, Anlaby Road and Sidmouth Street, killing twenty-five people and seriously injuring a further twenty-eight.[102]

The next raid, on 18 July, was the last heavy one of the year. Over 170 HEs and three GMs weighing 36 tons hit the area around Victoria Dock and along the banks of the River Hull.[103] One hundred and forty-three civilians died, along with three servicemen, and more than 100 were seriously injured.

At Rustenburg Street, an HE demolished six houses, including that of 42-year-old ARP volunteer Ernest Dead Hodgson. Upon investigating, he found that the Anderson Shelter of

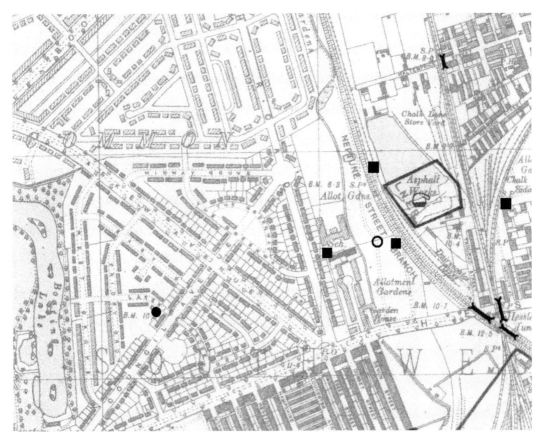

Francis Askew School was hit on 11 July 1941, while a second high-explosive bomb landed on the nearby railway embankment. The unexploded parachute mine between them and the high-explosive bombs to the north and east were part of an earlier raid. The parachute mine detonation on Council Avenue to the west was on 25 April 1941.

Damage to Francis Askew School.

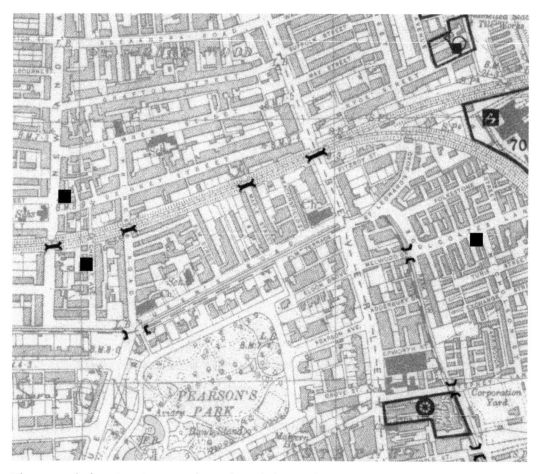

The west end of De Grey Street was hit in the early hours of 15 July 1941.

The location today. (Courtesy of Barnaby Cooper)

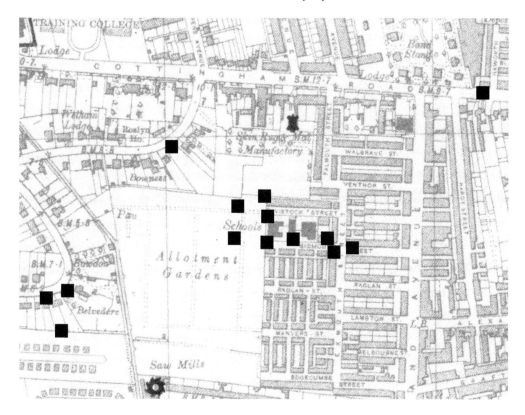

*Above*: Sidmouth Street
saturated with high explosives
on 15 July 1941.

*Right*: A post-war infill on
Sidmouth Street. (Courtesy of
Barnaby Cooper)

his neighbour, a Mrs Pounder, had been tipped over and covered in debris. Working unaided
for some twenty minutes, Hodgson managed to release Mrs Pounder and her three children.
The City Engineer later testified:

> This work was done in the midst of other bombs falling in neighbouring streets, and the amount
> of debris moved for one man was considerable. In fact, as Mr Hodgson says, he did not know

his own strength that night. This rescue is all the more creditable when it is realised that two men wearing steel helmets shouted at him to ask if he needed assistance, but promptly disappeared and did not return when another bomb came whistling down in the immediate vicinity.[104]

Hodgson received an official commendation for his efforts.[105]

The nearest FAP to Rustenburg Street was in Morrill Street, where yet again Dr Wilson and his staff worked efficiently and tirelessly to cope with the stream of casualties. On that night, a total of 163 patients passed through the FAP,[106] yet ironically the only person to die there was a member of staff, when an HE exploded in the street outside. Dr Wilson later recalled:

> ... all the doors of the first-aid post were blown down, and we had to keep sticking the black-out up again. Not long afterwards two pieces of the street were hurled onto the roof [by an explosion in New Bridge Road] along with a 'Buses stop here' sign.

Dr Wilson was appointed a Member of the Order of the British Empire for his actions on 18 July and during the heavy raids in May.[107]

At around 02:25 three HEs disabled most of the fire-fighting equipment at Spillers Ltd's Swan Mills, and set the building alight. When an AFS unit arrived, it was unable to connect to the city water supply, so 49-year-old mill manager Charles Mander Stanton suggested using the well under the fitting shop, which held 22,000 gallons (100,000 litres). Forty-one-year-old employee James Snitch, with the assistance of Herbert Baggeley, attempted to reach the valve to turn it on, but were beaten back by flames and falling debris. Snitch then tried again, along with 43-year-old John Henry Slater, but found the area dense with smoke, and that a 120ft water tower had collapsed around the valve. On the third attempt, Snitch, Slater and Stanton cleared away large quantities of bricks, rubble and wood to reach the valve, which they succeeded in turning on, allowing the use of the water to fight the fire. Snitch and Slater were awarded the British Empire Medal, while Stanton received an official commendation.[108] [109] [110]

At George Street the LNER Control Offices were hit, collapsing the building and trapping five firewatchers. A rescue party led by 37-year-old John Joseph McHugh was first on the scene at around 01:45, and they set to work driving a shaft into the east side of the debris. Thirty-eight-year-old George Arthur Dixon was at the forefront of this effort, which resulted in the release of the first of the firewatchers alive. This was despite the ongoing attack, a fierce fire nearby from a ruptured gas main, and the presence of an unexploded bomb in the area.[111]

At this point a second rescue party, led by F. Furling, arrived, and he agreed with McHugh that his team would start tunnelling from the west side of the debris to maximise the chance of finding the remaining firewatchers.[112] A second man was the next to be rescued alive by Dixon, barely an hour into the operation, but the work became increasingly heavy-going, although the bombing ceased around 04:15.[113] The third firewatcher was reached at 07:45, but he was already dead.[114]

On the west side, 37-year-old Enoch Emmerson Jacklin – who had worked so hard to save the life of the 11-year-old girl at Blenheim Street on 3 June – led the tunnelling efforts, and at around 09:00 located 63-year-old firewatcher Alfred Beckett. Furling later reported:

> A tunnel was driven into the unstable debris and after hours of dangerous and tiring work carried out in the main by volunteer Jacklin, one of the missing persons, a firewatcher named Beckitt [sic], was reached. This man was not only buried beneath tons of debris but was also trapped by huge baulks of timber.
>
> As volunteer Jacklin was approaching the man Beckitt, a delayed action bomb went off in the neighbourhood and caused Jacklin to be buried temporarily by debris dislodged by the earth tremor. Other members of the rescue parties present quickly realised the position and Jacklin was himself released...[115]

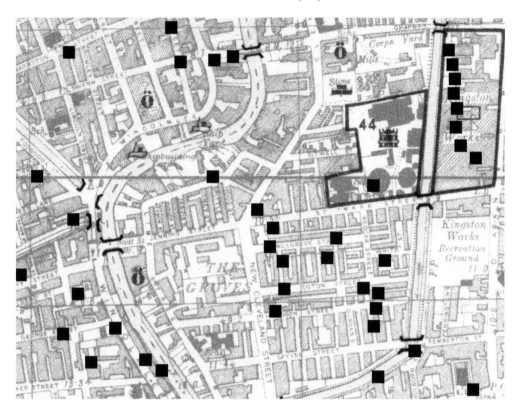

The area around Mulgrave Street – at the centre of the map – was hit on 18 July 1941, resulting in a great loss of life. The aircraft was probably trying to hit the industrial targets to the north, which included a gasworks.

Beckett was released at around 10:15, some eight and half hours after the start of rescue operations, but died in hospital a week later. The last body was not recovered until the afternoon of 20 July.[116] For his actions Dixon was awarded the George Medal, while McHugh and Jacklin each received the British Empire Medal.[117] [118]

Destroyed on 18 July 1941, Nos 87–89 George Street were the LNER Control Offices.

The former Young People's Institute survives on the left. (Courtesy of Barnaby Cooper)

As heavy as the raid of 18 July was, the destruction within Hull could have been even worse were it not for the ultimate outcome of Major Calvert-Jones' visit to Denham Studios in 1937. The Air Ministry has realised the potential for diverting night attacks on its own airfields by constructing decoy sites in the likely path of attacking bombers, and in time the theory was applied not only to other military facilities but also to industrial ones, and even whole towns. Lights were used to simulate key features, as if poorly blacked out, while various fire effects mimicked the targets as if they were already ablaze.

By 1941 Hull benefited from no less than six such sites. Large fire decoys were known as SF or Starfish sites, and there were two outside the villages of Ganstead and Bilton to represent Hull itself. QF sites were decoys simulating different types of fire and/or smoke, such as from burning and collapsing buildings, while QL were a fire variation meant to suggest a burning oil installation, and there was one such near Paull to mimic the oil storage tanks at Salt End. There were combined Naval SF/QF sites at Paull Home Sands, Little Humber and Thorney Crofts. The SF element of the latter was no less than an immense series of concrete tanks or basins – illuminated by electric lights hung above them – on the Humber foreshore at Cherry Cobb Sands, arranged to represent the partial outline of the Alexandra and King George Docks.

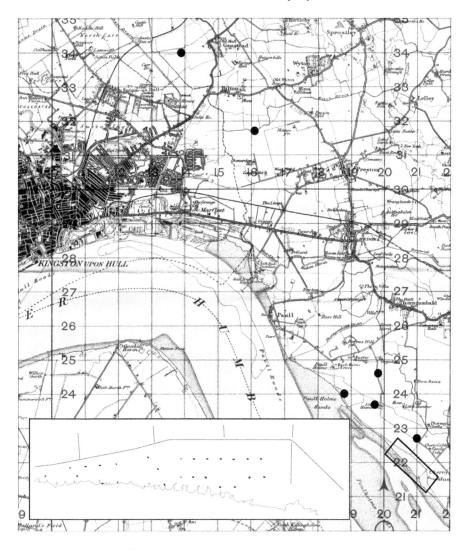

Decoy sites around Hull, from top:

Ganstead [TA 139340]: SF
Bilton [TA 161317]: SF
Paull [TA 198246]: QF
Paull Home Sands [TA 188240] SF/QL
Little Humber [TA 197237] SF/QL
Thorney Croft [TA 210227] SF/QL
Outline of Cherry Cobb Sands docks decoy

The docks decoy mimics features of both Alexandra and King George Dock, along with the curved railway inbetween. For the King George part, an envelope-shaped trapezoid to the north-west is often suggested as representing the lock gates, yet the presence of a corresponding one to the south-east instead indicates that they are supposed to be the inside corners of the tail of the original T-shaped form of the dock.

There had been recriminations when the decoys had not been activated during the heavy raids in May, mainly because the sites had not been notified quickly enough when the attacks started, or – in Hull's case – not notified at all. There was better luck during the 18 July raid, when the Naval SF sites were targeted with a small number of HEs, which would otherwise have dropped on Hull.[119]

The sheer scale of May and July's heavy raids were a cause for concern for the national authorities, and a number of secret reports were compiled assessing how Hull had coped on each occasion.[120] Generally it was thought that the city had held up well, although the casualty and mortuary service had exhibited severe failings, particularly after the July raid. It was also noted that amongst the civilian population there were

> …many expressions of opinion regarding recent statements made by the Prime Minister in which he adopted a challenging attitude towards the Nazis, as, for instance, when he called upon them to, 'Do their worst.' While there appears to be no lack of courage on the part of the people, some seem to be under the impression that such speeches are an incitement, the consequences of which are borne by the civilian population.[121]

The final raid of July saw just five HEs and three PMs scattered across Holderness Road, Holland Street and Preston Road in the early hours of the 23rd.[122] The PMs landed in Alexandra Dock, arming themselves as naval mines rather than exploding.[123] One went off later in the day, killing an elderly couple. Again the Naval SFs did their job, attracting maybe as many HEs as actually hit Hull during the raid.[124]

Following the heavy raids in May, the Great War practice of civilians trekking to outlying areas made a comeback. Many of the districts in which they sought nightly refuge were not unwelcoming, but the authorities in Hull did their best to discourage it. Following the heavy raid on the night of 18/19 July the daily exodus only increased. On 21 July the Chief Warden and current Sheriff, Robert Greenwood Tarran, decided to investigate personally. Parking his car about a mile from the village of Bilton – a known destination for trekkers – he adopted the disguise of a working man's outfit, and walked to the centre of the village. He later reported to the Corporation:

> After walking up to what is more or less the centre of the village near the Church and talking to many folk and asking about billets and if I could get a blanket, I eventually was directed to the Piggery by a man and two women, who were most considerate in showing me and guiding me there.
> I eventually found room in one of the pig sties in the Piggery and apologised to the families who were in this sty, for disturbing them and asked if they minded me joining them. Then with my respirator as my pillow and my light rug, I lay down on the straw. In this up to date pig sty each sty or pen had its own lavatory accommodation at the back – for the pigs – which was constantly used as I was to find out later by both sexes during the night.[125]

People began to fall asleep, but after about an hour the air-raid siren sounded and several men got up and went outside to act as firewatchers, returning when the all-clear sounded half an hour later.

> After about half an hour when everything had been very quiet the rats started. I seemed to have chosen the place which was a traffic road for the rats. Probably that was why no-one was sleeping there. They ran over me, then ran under me, but seeing that there were children in the same pig sty as myself, I kept very quiet for fear anything I did would waken the children and they would become scared. Slowly I heard rustling of straw in other pig sties and a man would say to a woman very quietly, 'There's rats.' Gradually

the talk of rats became more audible until the inhabitants of the pig sty talked to the inhabitants of another. One man said there were a couple who'd been doing a dance on him. Someone from another pen said, 'There has been one running across me with clogs on.' From another pen a woman's voice said, 'Well, never mind, I would sooner have British rats than Hitler's bombs.'[126]

In the morning Tarran joined the start of the 4-mile walk back to Hull, hearing the complaints and concerns of the trekkers:

No buses, nothing to give them a lift of any description, all moaning because there was no refreshment, no warm drink, no opportunity of fresh milk for their babies, but there was not a scrap of demoralised feeling. They were fighting fit, pleased to have had a night's rest, the men folk especially, and the mothers. It did seem pitiable that the Ministry of Health of this country should allow the young children to be doing those miles there each night and morning, with only a few hours' sleep, which while it is all that grown up people need, it is only half what children need.[127]

He then slipped away, returning to his car and losing his disguise, and headed back to the city, picking up some of the trekkers in the process. He subsequently provided his building firm's lorries free of charge to transport the trekkers, and eventually more organised and officially sanctioned measures were put in place.

Later in the year it was found more expedient to use schools on the outskirts of the city as rest centres for those women and children from the most at-risk areas. Around the docks in particular, where 90 per cent of the housing had been damaged, workers were insistent that their families be kept safe while they continued working.

Throughout the war the British authorities were concerned not only with what effect their own bombing campaign was having on German civilians, but also how British civilians were coping with Luftwaffe attacks. Researching this issue fell to the Ministry of Home Security (MoHS), which continuously surveyed and monitored selected British towns and cities to try to gauge how morale was holding up – or not, as the case may be.

To this end, one imaginative idea was to have Hull's teachers set their pupils (many of whom had returned after the evacuation of 1939) an essay on the subject of 'What I Did in an Air Raid' in early 1942. Most of the results have now been lost, although a cache of twenty-nine essays by girls from Springburn Street School was rediscovered in 2014,[128] while others survive in MoHS files. Thirteen-year-old Margaret Bielby of Villa Place Senior Girls' School wrote about a raid in March 1941:

As I entered the shelter I heard the warden say to another man, 'Three bombs have fallen on Lister Street near the stables.' This made my heart leap as I lived next door to the stables. Next I heard a plane, and a crash, then I heard someone shout 'Duck.' I did not know a high explosive bomb had struck the shelter until I woke up and found myself in a strange house, covered with bruises and scratches.[129]

On the night of 7/8 May, Margaret was in the shelter at Lister Street when their neighbours' house, belonging to the Dove family, was bombed:

The time was nearly four o'clock when a bomb dropped on the shelter, and when I recovered I was in the Children's Hospital with Mrs Dove and Alice. The rest of the family was buried, and later on they died. Many people thought I was dead, but in spite of air raids I am all right.[130]

A pupil at Craven Street Senior School, 11-year-old Edward Greensides recalled an Oil Bomb dropping on Abbey Street on the night of 8/9 May, while he and his family were in the shelter at White's Sugar Mill in Williamson Street:

> A warden came in and said that the mill was on fire. The women saying, 'If we get caught in here what shall we do?' but the men tried to cheer them up. When all of us were talking we saw smoke coming from a corner of the shelter and I thought we were all going to suffocate. While we were watching the smoke it was getting thicker and getting into each corner, so the warden called for the men to open the iron [escape] trap door with him. When they had opened it, the warden told us to climb up the ladder and get on top as quickly as we could. When we were on top, we saw big telegraph poles burning.[131]

Thirteen-year-old Sydney Chapman described an adventurous night during one of the May 1941 raids. Initially sheltering with his family, he went to check on an aunt when they heard a bomb drop in the next street. When he arrived at her house an IB landed in the garden, so he covered it with sand and then checked that his aunt was alright. Returning to the shelter, he heard someone say St Charles' Church had been hit by IBs, so he went to investigate, finding that it was actually Ansteys the drapers on the corner of Charles Street and Jarratt Street.

> When I was watching the fire, a bomb dropped and the blast knocked a piece of burning timber into the second-hand shop next door, so I went and told a fireman who broke the back door down with his axe and put out the fire with a hosepipe. As he was walking out of the back passage he saw a man looting in Gowies the watchmakers and jewellers, so he went and got hold of him, and gave him to a policeman, who took him to the police station. After that I went to see the damage on Ferensway. There I saw the Bus Station on fire and firemen trying to out it with hosepipes and chemical extinguishers.[132]

He then described seeing fire-fighting and salvage work at Hammonds, Bladons and Thornton Varley's on Prospect Street, and elsewhere. He then returned home, had a cup of tea, then went out again, until the all-clear sounded at 04:45. Returning home for breakfast, he then went to collect the newspapers for his round from WH Smith at Paragon station. After completing his round,

> I went down Worship Street. As I was half way down the street an unexploded bomb went off killing three people, a man and two ladies. The blast from the bomb knocked me down and broke the church windows. When I got up I felt dizzy, so two firemen took me to a Mobile Canteen Van, where I had a cup of tea to steady my head. When I had drunk my tea I thanked the firemen and went home. When I got home I helped my Mother to clear the debris out of the back yard and clear the debris out of the front garden and off the front path. When I finished that, I went to bed till half past four in the afternoon.[133]

# Chapter 5
# Finale: August 1941 to March 1945

King George VI and Queen Elizabeth II visited Hull on 5 August 1941, touring bomb-damaged areas, and meeting civil defence workers and volunteers, and civilians. They visited recently hit residential areas – including Mulgrave Street – and industrial sites. The *Hull Daily Mail* reported:

> Commenting on the Hull raids, the King said: 'It is very brave of the people to stand up to them so well.' He told the Regional Commissioner, Lieutenant-General Sir William Bartholomew, that he was deeply impressed by the cheerful spirit of the people.[1]

On 8 August, although no bombs were dropped, the Luftwaffe was active over Hull. 944 Balloon Squadron reported a single enemy aircraft flying low but in cloud over the city during an alert between 14:48 and 15:16,[2] but there may have been more. Certainly one Dornier Do 217 failed to return, and is thought to have crashed in the Humber.[3]

On the same day the *Aufklärungsgruppe (Fern)* had despatched a single Messerschmitt BF 110C long-range fighter on reconnaissance over Hull, which was subsequently shot down by two Spitfires of 129 (Mysore) Squadron from Leconfield when it was spotted heading west towards a convoy off Flamborough Head, but this was some two hours before the

George VI and Queen Elizabeth visited Hull on 5 August 1941.

Prime Minister Winston Churchill in the city later in the year.

944 Squadron report. The two crew were seen to survive the ditching, but appear to have drowned subsequently.[4]

There was a medium-sized HE-only raid in the early hours of 18 August, across east and central Hull.[5] Nineteen people were killed, including one serviceman at home, and a Merchant Seaman.

Two shops and five houses were demolished at the corner of Holborn Mount and Pemberton Street. ARP Warden W. Ward, knowing where the occupants usually sheltered, set about trying to find them, and assisted by a warden by the name of Noble and 44-year-old PWR Constable Harold Ellwood, got seven people out of a shelter behind the houses. Ward later reported:

> I then located the people trapped in the basement and under the debris of No. 4 [Holborn Mount], and PWR 898 Ellwood, assisted by PC 461 Green and Warden Noble, commenced to dig down, and after further sawing several beams we located Michael Robinson, 4 years, and his father [Arthur Robinson].
>
> We got the boy out alright, but owing to Robinson senior being trapped by debris PWR 898 Ellwood volunteered to go underneath. Whilst we held the beams of wood Ellwood worked his way under the debris which was in danger of collapsing all the time.
>
> All this time the smell of coal gas was getting stronger, but Ellwood carried on, and was successful in releasing Robinson, and then passed him along with his daughter Elsie, 3 years, through the opening to us and after rendering First Aid, we had to pull Ellwood out from the debris owing to him having been overcome by coal gas fumes.[6]

Ellwood received an official commendation for his actions.[7]

On the night of 31 August/1 September, between twenty and twenty-fire enemy aircraft concentrated on Hull, East Yorkshire, and North Lincolnshire.[8] On this occasion the Hull SF site at Bilton was activated in time, attracting at least forty HEs.[9] The best measure of this success is the fact that – in contrast – only fifteen bombs were recorded across Hull,[10] a total of 7 tons, which nevertheless killed forty-six people, twenty-nine of them at Waterloo Terrace, Wellington Lane. More than thirty people were seriously injured, and sixteen air-raid shelters were damaged.

The last three raids of 1941 – on 21 September, 12/13 October, and 7/8 November – were relatively minor. The first was five 50kg HEs and a single IB cluster, while the other

The corner of Harley Street and Beverley Road, demolished in the autumn of 1941.

The Salvation Army centre on the same site today. (Courtesy of Barnaby Cooper)

**FIREBOMB FRITZ will come again Are you ready to put him out?**

YES! Britain's Fire Guard — we men and women of Britain — are resolved and ready to save our factories, our railways, our food, our homes.

Fire Guard work is often dull, sometimes dangerous, but it's a job that's got to be done. Our heart and soul is in it. We train and we practise. We know our sectors like the backs of our hands — every corner, every roof top. We watch. We climb ladders, work pumps, wield sandbags.

We will shatter Firebomb Fritz, and all the Nazi horrors he stands for.

**FIRE GUARD TIPS. No. 1.**
*Firebombs that fall in the street are usually harmless unless they are close to something inflammable, like a motor vehicle. Look for bombs on buildings first.*

**BRITAIN SHALL NOT BURN!**

ISSUED BY THE MINISTRY OF HOME SECURITY

The Firebomb Fritz adverts ran in the national and regional press from September to November 1941.

two were both just four 500kg HEs. No one is known to have died, with only two people seriously injured in October.[11]

At 11:40 on 4 December a Miles Master advanced trainer (serial W8595) hit one of 942 Squadron's barrage balloon's cables, and crashed in Dover Street, bursting into flames and destroying three houses. The pilot, a Flight Sergeant F.H.R. Hulbert (742801), bailed out and landed safely by parachute.[12] Many years later he recalled that members of 942 Squadron personnel – who were naturally interested in the result of an aircraft hitting one of their balloon cables (even if not an enemy!) – took him to the crash site. To Hulbert's recollection his aircraft had come down 'in the gardens of a row of already bombed out houses and all that remained of it was the tail wheel – the aircraft had exploded with about three quarters of a tank full of aviation spirit on board.'[13]

The west side of Dover Street had indeed been hit by two HEs during the heavy May 1941 raids – at Nos 1–3 and 41–43. Hulbert's aircraft, however, came down in the middle, demolishing Nos 17 and 19, and leaving No. 15 with a cut-down upper storey and a flat roof. Local folklore has it that the flat roof was intended as a temporary measure that was never subsequently replaced.[14]

The pre-war prototype of the Miles Master trainer that crashed on Dover Street in December 1941. (Courtesy of Ernie Cooper)

The truncated house in Dover Street with its 'temporary' flat roof, flanked by a post-war infill. (Courtesy of Barnaby Cooper)

With a sad inevitability the practice of sending white feathers to those judged – usually incorrectly – by others to be shirking their duty made a reappearance. One such recipient in February 1942 was 47-year-old Frederick George Smith, a Merchant Navy Third Engineer. The *Hull Daily Mail* reported that Smith:

> …has been going to seas for seven years, including an almost unbroken spell of 18 months since the war began, during which time he has been bombed and seen his ship attacked by torpedoes. His engagement finished, he came home for a spell to join the pool of merchant seamen waiting for a new vessel, and was granted the normal leave which he has a right to enjoy.[15]

It was further stated that Smith was keen to meet whoever had sent him the feather, with the newspaper furnishing his full address, and, 'his fighting weight: 12st.-odd.' On 25 September Smith's ship the SS *Boston* was torpedoed and sunk. All the crew were picked up by the American SS *New Bedford*, which herself was torpedoed and sunk on 20 October, with the loss of all hands and all but two of the *Boston*'s crew, neither being Smith.[16] [17]

On the night of 8/9 March, *Kampfgeschwader 2* despatched a force of 107 bombers to attack industrial installations and port facilities in Hull, from which one Dornier 217E failed to return, with the loss of its four-man crew, whose bodies were never recovered.[18] No bombs were dropped on Hull itself, although 942/943 Balloon Squadron reported: 'Gun fire and bombs reported to the East and North East of Site 48.' This was between 20:15 and 23:02,[19] and Site 48 was at Northumberland Avenue. Seventeen Balloon Centre recorded that 465 anti-aircraft rounds were expended on the night, and that HEs were dropped at Cottingham, and PMs in the Humber.[20] On the night of 13/14 April what must have been just one aircraft dropped three HEs, killing seven people.[21]

The early hours of 1 May saw a single German bomber approach the city from the south at 3,000ft (915m), then turn back to drop three 500kg bombs as it flew back south at 03:35, straddling the railway track south of Botanic Gardens junction. The first bomb landed to the west of the railway, causing some damage to the track, and the second to the rear of a house on the north side of Bank Street. Seven people were killed at Nos 26 and 28 Bank Street, with an eighth dying in hospital three days later.

Although Bank Street and Victoria Street had originally been constructed around 1890 as residential terraces, by 1942 a bakery belonging to William Jackson occupied the west end of the south and north sides of the streets, respectively. In addition, two of the houses on Victoria Street (Nos 2 and 4) had been replaced with an associated creamery, and the third bomb landed directly behind this. There were a number of concrete and/or brick domestic and works shelters – for both the creamery and the bakery – which suffered various degrees of damage. Fortunately, the domestic shelters were unoccupied at the time.[22]

Thirty-nine-year-old George Arthur Ryder, the chief officer of the Jackson's works' fire brigade, found five people in the creamery shelter, four of whom he led to safety, whilst carrying the fifth. He then returned to the building to turn off the water main, a risky task with numerous severed live electricity cables. He then struggled to turn off the leaking gas main, which had been buried by the collapsed roof. He was partly overcome by the poisonous coal gas, but managed to shut it off and get out of the building. Once outside, he returned to the main bakery, where he collapsed and passed out, only regaining consciousness after being admitted to the Hull Royal Infirmary.[23] He was subsequently awarded the British Empire Medal.[24]

On the night of 19/20 May a force of 132 aircraft of *Luftflotte 3* was sent to attack Hull, of which around 100 reported finding the target. A Dornier 217 and two Junkers 882 failed to return from the raid.[25] In all, seventy-four assorted HEs weighing over 33 tons were dropped, along with four clusters of IBs, yet the casualties were surprisingly light, totalling forty-seven in all.[26] [27]

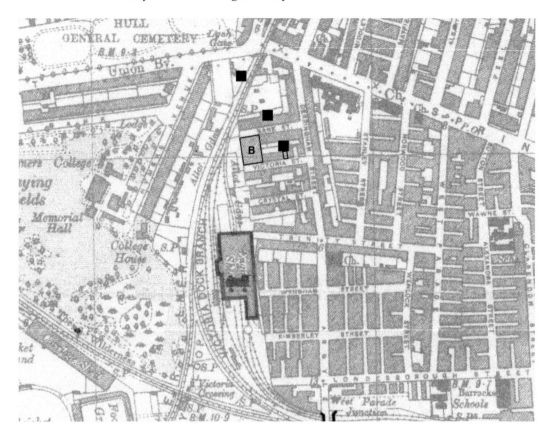

High-explosive bombs near Botanic Junction on 1 May 1942. The 'B' indicates the Jacksons Bakery, and, outlined to the right, the associated creamery. Jacksons still occupies the same site – now much expanded – to this day.

Around 00:15 on the 20th, Warden John William Collins, on his way to his post, spotted IBs dropping around Ripon Street, off Hedon Road.[28] Investigating further, he encountered 42-year-old Charles Andrews, an ostler at the LNER's stables, which were on fire. Andrews went inside to release the horses, so that Collins could lead them to a picket line 30 yards (27m) from the fire, or to wagons in the yard. At one point an IB landed nearby and started another fire, which Collins smothered with the contents of a sandbag before going back to the horses. Just as the last horses were being led out of the building, the roof collapsed onto the now empty stalls. Collins reported: 'Had it not been that I am an ex-Horse Artillery man, I could not possibly have dealt with the more nervous horses, which were roaring and kicking.'[29]

With the horses – two dozen in all – safe, the two men began to tackle the blaze using the LNER's equipment, until the arrival of the National Fire Service at 00:45.

Initially Collins was recommended for official recognition, but as this was being considered the issue arose of whether Andrews was equally deserving. Inspector J.W.M. Davison stated:

From my own experience of terrified horses, I am satisfied that Collins is worthy of recognition, for while Andrews' conduct would be equally courageous, he would have the advantage of knowing the horses and being known by them, whilst Collins was entirely strange to them, although I am told that he has a fair knowledge of handling horses.

I have no hesitation in saying that in my opinion Collins acted in a most courageous manner, showing a disregard for his own personal safety and a keen devotion to his duty as an Air Raid Warden.[30]

Both men received official commendations. [31]

Near St Andrew's Dock, a single HE hit the north end of Scarborough Street, which at the time was mainly residential, with a number of side terraces and a school in the middle. Twenty-four people were killed, and many others were left trapped under the debris of the houses. At the forefront of the recovery operation was 37-year-old Dr Robert Hamilton Moyes, who repeatedly and at great personal risk gave aid to those trapped. Moyes had succeeded Dr Diamond as the city's Deputy Medical Officer of Health after the latter was killed in 1941. Dr N. Beggie, the Medical Officer of Health, reported:

[Moyes] rendered assistance to many people trapped at various places throughout the area of this widespread incident, and gave morphia to ease the suffering of those who could not be immediately released. This necessitated his crawling into tunnels on two occasions at a time when debris was still falling and there was considerable risk of personal injury. He carried on with his humanitarian efforts regardless of personal risk and displayed a high degree of courage. His initiative and skill undoubtedly saved several lives, brought much needed comfort to the suffering, and his calm demeanour was an inspiration to all.[32]

Subsequently fifty local residents signed a request that Dr Moyes' actions be officially recognised, and he was later appointed a Member of the Order of the British Empire (MBE).[33]

At 00:20 an HE exploded near the Pickering Almshouses, demolishing two of the houses and trapping three residents inside. First on the scene was Sergeant Baker of the City Police, and 40-year-old civilian Arnold Ernest Bateson. While Baker assisted an elderly couple by the name of Cooper, Bateson searched for a Mrs Morgan. It was later reported:

Without hesitation, Bateson climbed through a blown-out window, contacted Mrs Morgan and started to remove the rubble and brick from her head and shoulders: at this time the roof was hanging from the adjoining house and likely to fall at any moment. During all this period, at great personal risk, Bateson continued to clear debris and remove material from her body.

He worked himself under the debris and at the same time held up a wall, by this action protecting Mrs Morgan from further injury. Although ordered to come out by a rescue party, he refused to remove himself until the wall was propped up. Afterwards, he still insisted on rendering such assistance as was in his power, and did not leave until the woman had been extricated.[34]

Bateson was awarded the British Empire Medal.[35]

In the early hours of 1 August, an 1,800kg bomb descended on Grindell Street, close to Alexandra Dock. Today the road is lined with industrial units, but at the time it was terraces of workers' houses. The bomb obliterated Nos 2–5 Grindell Street to the north, and part of Malabar Terrace, Churchill Street to the south. In Churchill Street, twenty-three people died, comprising between two and seven members each of the Noble, Ryalls, Newland and Inman/Stephenson families, and one man in Malabar Terrace.

The first rescue party on the scene was led by 51-year-old foreman John Christopher Staveley, who immediately set to work releasing a young girl trapped under the wreckage. The City Engineer reported:

The child was trapped beneath the wreckage of the buildings. The removal of the child was a delicate matter and all who saw the operation commented on the manner in which

Staveley spoke to the girl in order to win her confidence so that she would carry out his suggestions in such a manner as to simplify the complicated job of extricating her.[36]

Alderman J.L. (Leo) Schultz was on the scene and stated, 'I strongly recommend Foreman Staveley for an award for his coolness, devotion to duty, and personal disregard of danger.'[37]

Although put forward for a British Empire Medal, the fact that the air raid had ceased at the time of the rescue meant that Staveley instead received an official commendation.[38]

There was a minor attack on 24/25 October, with seven HEs resulting in a single death and at least six people seriously injured,[39] but on 18 November there was a more indirect loss of life. Thirty-seven-year-old Firewatcher Thomas William Connaughton collapsed and died shortly after taking part in an ARP exercise involving crawling through a smoke-filled shelter to simulate a rescue of a trapped or unconscious person.[40] A subsequent inquest ruled the cause of death as heart disease accelerated by partial asphyxiation during the exercise. The Coroner, Dr A.G. Minn, stated:

> There is no doubt about it that this man is just as much a victim of Hitler as any man on the front line to-day. The evidence is quite clear – there is no evidence of any neglect on the part of the instructors or the Civil Defence.[41]

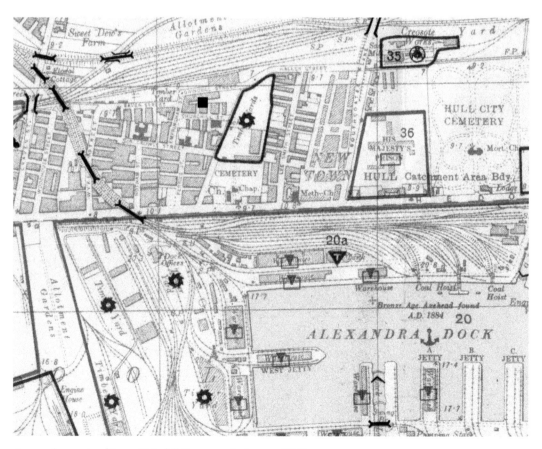

A parachute mine hit on Grindell Street on 1 August 1942.

The sixth and final raid of 1942 saw seven HEs on the night of 20/21 December, with the loss of three lives, along with ten seriously injured.[42] The overall death toll for the year was ninety-three – less than 10 per cent of the number in 1941.

Twenty-three German aircrafts were allocated to attack Hull on the night of 3/4 January 1943, although only fifteen made it to the target area, and only two 500kg HEs and nine clusters of IBs were recorded as falling in the city. A length of timber wharf was destroyed,

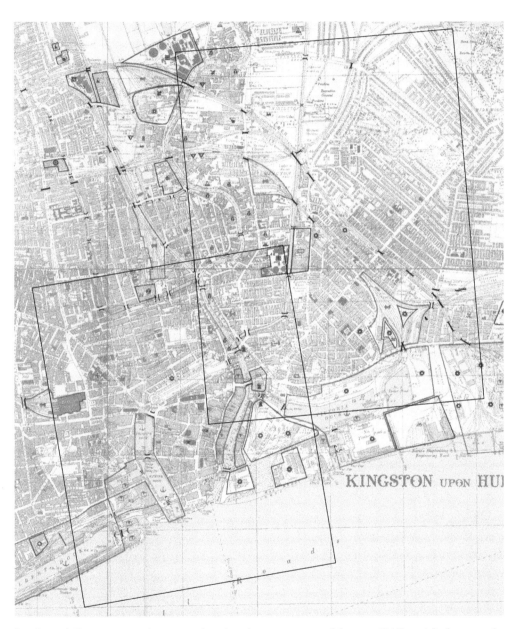

Portion of German targeting map, showing the areas covered by two RAF aerial photographs taken in 1943, shown on the next two pages.

but there were no deaths or serious injuries.[43] One Dornier 17 was damaged over Spurn Head whilst in-bound, and crash-landed at Skeffling (all four crew were taken prisoner), while a second was so damaged that it crashed on the Dutch coast during its return.[44]

On 26 April tragedy struck the 17 Balloon Centre when a gale swept across the seaborne barrage off Grimsby, with the loss of balloons from the drifters *Thora*, *Creag Mhor*, *Liberty*, *Student Prince*, and *Cleon*. The *Thora* fouled the defensive boom, began to sink, and was abandoned by the crew, with the loss of the skipper, George Beet, and AC1 Thomas Wrightman. Balloons at a number of the land sites were also lost or damaged.[45]

*Above and Opposite*: Two 1943 RAF aerial photographs of bomb damage in Hull.

After an absence of five months the Luftwaffe returned to Hull on the night of 23/24 June with a small force of between thirteen and fifteen aircraft. One was seen to carry out a diving attack from 5,000ft to 1,500ft (1,500m to 450m) before releasing its bombs, but the rest remained in level flight between 5,000ft and 8,000ft (1,500m and 2,400m).[46] Bombs – twenty HEs and eight IB clusters – were dropped across a wide area, including on Paragon station and the docks.[47]

Twenty-two civilians were killed on the night, plus two more from their injuries later, five at Carden Avenue, where 38-year-old rescue party foreman Thomas Richard Gale led the tunnelling into the rubble of a demolished house to reach a Mrs Venn, and one of her two children. Rescue party supervisor W.E. Purling later reported:

Mrs Venn [then] informed Foreman Gale that another child was trapped in the meter cupboard, and I could see that it would be necessary to tunnel some 8 or 10 feet from the point where the first persons were rescued, to reach the child. Foreman Gale elected to undertake this work, being the smallest member of his party. I could see that this was a hazardous operation, because not only was there danger of collapse, but a live electric cable crossed the line he must tunnel. Foreman Gale hand-picked his way into the debris and at one period I could only see the soles of his boots. When he was able to get his arms around the child, he called back for two of his party to take hold of his feet and drag him out. This, however, proved too great a strain, together with the fact that debris was cutting through his clothing into his body. He comforted the child, wriggled out backwards, collected a blanket and went in again, and rolling the child in the blanket, he inched his way back, dragging blanket and child with him.[48]

Gale had previously been unsuccessfully recommended for recognition for rescue work following the raid of 1 August 1942,[49] but on this occasion he was awarded the British Empire Medal.[50]

An internal Home Office report noted after the raid: 'Morale in Hull is good. The population accepts raiding as a necessary evil, but does not let it interfere with their work or play more than it must. There is a general air of levity.'[51]

One unexpected witness to the aftermath was the mathematician Dr Jacob Bronowski, who had previously taught at Hull University (and served as an Air Raid Warden) but at the time was employed by the Ministry of Home Security, and made a personal visit to the city in early July:

It was generally believed that anti-personnel bombs had been used, at least at Grimsby [on 13/14 June], in the shape of small pocket articles: the most popular were fountain pens, and the favourite colour was pink. Perhaps as a result of the campaign then in progress, these stories were most popular in the Wardens service. A less credulous warden assured me that, on the morning of the Hull raid, a pile of sandbags had in fact been erected round a pink fountain pen; this may be the highbrow form of the fountain pen rumour.

Equally widespread in and near Hull, especially among women, was the belief that anti-personnel bombs had been used at Grimsby in the shape of children's toys. Other version of the stories of such larger disguises were also current: the most circumstantial was that anti-personnel bombs had been used at Grimsby in the shape of books from the Grimsby Public Library, correct in all details of making and date-stamp.[52]

The 'anti-personnel bombs' used in both this raid and the one on Grimsby were actually the infamous SD2 'Butterfly' Bombs. These consisted of a 3.1-inch (6.2cm) long 3-inch (7.6cm) diameter drum encased in a sheet steel outer case that sprang open during descent, acting like a sycamore leaf to both arm the bomb and slow its descent. Scores could be dropped from a single aircraft, with a variety of fuses: some to explode on impact, after a set time-delay, or if moved on the ground. An indiscriminate booby-trap, they were often colourfully marked, making them irresistibly attractive to children.[53] [54] It is not known how many were dropped on Hull, but fourteen unexploded SD2s were found. They were all missing the outer casings, and as no dropping container was found, it was speculated that they may have been released by hand from the bombers.[55] [56]

Mobile laundry for those affected by bombing.

Women's Voluntary Service mobile canteen.

The last successful German attack of 1943 was on the night of 13/14 July, and one Luftwaffe pilot recalled the raid as being 'very tiring' because they had to fly very low to avoid the British radar.[57] Forty-seven HEs – almost all 500kg – were dropped, along with three clusters of IBs and thirty-five phosphorous bombs.[58] Twenty-eight people died on the ground, including six members of the same family in Trinity Street.

A single Dornier 217 was shot down, with the loss of its crew of four,[59] but they were not the only Luftwaffe casualties. A second Do 217 was shot up by a de Havilland Mosquito of 605 Squadron as it attempted to land at its base in the Netherlands; the aircraft was destroyed but the crew survived. Another Do 217 collided with a British night-fighter over Hull, and the bomber's wireless operator was thrown out of the aircraft.[60] [61] Whether he was killed by the initial impact or merely knocked unconscious and could not use his parachute is unknown, but his body was found at Sunk Island, and subsequently buried in Hull Northern Cemetery (see Appendix 2).

At Leonard Street, while heading for his post, 27-year-old part-time Air Raid Warden Ernest Wilson heard cries coming from a partially demolished house. Inside he found Arthur Henry Cherry still alive under some debris. With the help of someone else, Wilson freed Cherry and took him outside, where the man told him that his wife and 13-year-old daughter were still inside, trapped under a huge clump of clay thrown up from the bomb crater. Wilson, a manager for Burton's the tailors, was not a trained rescue worker, but rather than waiting for assistance he returned to the house and dug into the clay with his bare hands until he found Mrs Maud Annie Cherry's arm, working up to her face to find her still breathing. It was later reported:

> As Mrs Cherry was removed, the arm of the child became visible, and Wilson discovered that the child herself was under the wreckage of a lead water tank and the wreckage of an attic window frame; he knew she was already dead as he had felt her pulse. He worked on, however, and released the body, twisting her out with the help of some soldiers who had arrived. As the body was in a twisted position, he straightened it and then had to lie down as he felt violently ill.[62]

The Senior ARP Officer added:

> There seems little doubt that Wilson, who is epileptic, worked extremely hard without any regard for his own ill health, and kept a cool head, showed excellent leadership, and did not hesitate to attempt the release of people fastened in the wreckage in spite of the danger of further debris falling from the roof and the danger from the moving floor.[63]

Wilson then collapsed from exhaustion, but refused to go home and rest, instead staying on duty until 10:30 in the morning. For his actions he was awarded the British Empire Medal;[64] sadly Mrs Cherry died of her injuries two months later.

*Kampfgeschwader 2* attempted a large-scale attack on the night of 25/26 July, but while forty-seven of the fifty-one aircraft sent claimed to have reached Hull, a combination of mist, poor target marking and harassing British night-fighters meant that not a single bomb fell within the city boundary. Ten 1,000kg and eighty-eight 500kg HEs, and over 30,000 IBs were dropped to no appreciable effect. In return the Luftwaffe lost two Dornier 217s to a night-fighter of 605 Squadron while en route to Hull, off Spurn Head. Only two of the combined eight crew survived to be taken prisoner.[65] [66]

A third Do 217 was shot down by anti-aircraft fire during the attack, and crashed at Long Riston near Beverley with the loss of all four crew. They were buried in the graveyard of St Mary's Church in Brandesburton, near Hornsea,[67] alongside some of their compatriots who perished previously (see Appendix 2).

Rescue Squad workers comb through the rubble of a shattered home for signs of life.

Civil Defence workers take a break. Many of them had full-time jobs in addition to this vital work.

On the night of 21/22 September forty-nine aircrafts were detailed to mine-laying operations in the Humber. One Dornier Do 217, in attempting to engage the anti-aircraft defences near Withernsea, flew too low and crashed, killing its four-man crew.[68] They were later buried in Hull Northern Cemetery (see Appendix 2). The Dornier's bomb-load of mines failed to explode on impact, and two Royal Navy personnel were badly injured as they attempted to tackle them on the afternoon of the 22nd.[69]

On the night of 2/3 October a mixed force of fifty-six German aircraft were sent to carry out mine-laying operations in the Humber, of which forty-nine carried out their objective. One Junkers 188 crashed half a mile from the Spurn lighthouse, with the loss of all four crew,[70] who were subsequently buried in Hull Northern Cemetery (see Appendix 2).

The only recorded war-related death in Hull during 1944 resulted from an accident the previous year. On 11 October 1943, 56-year-old LNER Dockyard Fire Guard William Houldsworth Leaper was leaving the Docks when he accidentally cycled into the water. Rescued and given artificial respiration, he apparently recovered and returned to work a fortnight later, but was admitted to hospital in April 1944. A subsequent inquest determined that he died from toxaemia resulting from pneumonia, with the coroner recording a verdict of 'Accidental Death'.[71]

On 12 August, 52-year-old Air Raid Warden Henry McGuire was injured at Tarrans Recreation Ground. It was reported that McGuire, 'in the furtherance of his [ARP] duties,' was guiding children in 'aerial trapeze' at the recreation ground, when he fell, injuring his pelvis. He was hospitalised for nine days and appeared to be recovering after discharge home, but had a relapse of the acute bronchitis that developed after the injury, and died.[72][73]

Like most of northern England, Hull was largely spared the German V-weapon onslaught that began shortly after D-Day, with one single exception. Although generally despatched from a ground ramp, a method was devised of air-launching V1 Flying Bombs from Heinkel He 111 bombers. As part of an intended attack on Manchester, fifty Heinkels of *Kampfgeschwader 53* launched one V1 apiece as they crossed the Lincolnshire coast between Skegness and Mablethorpe in the early hours of 24 December. The missiles were supposed to fly almost exactly due east towards Lancashire, but nineteen either crashed immediately or went astray. At least four veered north, with the first ending up harmlessly in the Humber, and the rest crashing at Willerby and South Cliffe (both at 05:45), and Pocklington (at 05:50).[74] The Willerby V1 landed close to the Hull Corporation's Springhead Pumping Station, causing extensive damage to both it and nearby houses.[75]

On 2 March 1945 the *Hull Daily Mail* reported: 'At last we have come to the stage where the great German military machine is slowly but unmistakably breaking down.'[76]

Despite this prediction, one or more enemy aircraft roamed across Hull in the early hours of 4 March, indiscriminately firing cannon shells, with hits reported in no less than twenty-two different locations.[77] The sheer pointlessness of this attack seemed to underscore the fact that the Luftwaffe had become no more than a minor irritant, but there was still one last throw of the dice to come.

It was a clear evening on 17 March, and the streets were by no means deserted. Few people even bothered to look up as the single aircraft droned overhead. Germany, after all, was finished. The Luftwaffe had few aeroplanes left, and virtually no fuel. With Allied forces bearing down on the last pockets of Nazi resistance, who could possibly think that it had the resources – let alone the will – to bomb any part of the UK, let alone battered old Kingston upon Hull?

The aircraft swooped down and a large number of SD10 Fragmentation Bombs were dropped. Compared to what Hull had previously been on the receiving end of, these were small: only 21.5 inches (54.6cm) in length and 3.4 inches (8.6cm) in diameter, but packed with a huge number of 7mm (0.28 inch) steel cubes set in concrete. When the bomb exploded, these pre-formed fragments – along with the shredded bomb casing – flew in all directions like a hail of bullets.[78]

Crossing Sherburn Street, 71-year-old John Reed tried to shield a boy from the shrapnel, but both of them died. Second-Lieutenant Stanley Duncan of the Royal Northumberland Fusiliers, home on leave, was also killed. In all, twelve people died in the street or were mortally wounded, and twenty-two hospitalised, with one woman dying of her injuries four days later.[79] Some of the casualties had been taken by bystanders to Morrill Street FAP, but it had long since ceased to operate.

There can have been no possible thought that the raid had any real military purpose, and in fact the 'choice' of munitions may simply reflect all that was still available, along with the aircraft itself. Even so, it is hard not to recognise that it would have taken an extreme form of determination for the crew to fly into the teeth of overwhelming Allied air superiority to deliver one last gesture of defiance. Whether it was down to courage or fanaticism, we shall never know, but it was the last raid on the UK by piloted enemy aircraft of the war.

Salvage and recyling was a major part of the war effort, but also a tempting target for looters. The *Hull Daily Mail* carried regular reports of those caught helping themselves to scrap metal, building materials, or firewood.

# Chapter 6
# Railway, Industrial and Infrastructure Damage

### 19/20 June 1940
A High Explosive (HE) bomb on or near the Chapman Street Bridge over the Foredyke Stream demolished part of the parapet.[1][2] Clear by 05:40 on the 20th.[3] Another HE damaged the nearby East Hull Gas Company's private railway siding, but did not affect the main LNER tracks.[4] Normal working resumed during the 20th.[5]

At 09:20 on the 20th an unexploded bomb (UXB) was reported on the side of the railway tracks between the Dansom Lane and Holderness Road level crossings. Hull City police officers were standing by pending removal, but trains still running through.[6] Removed at 11:30.[7]

### 25/26 June 1940
Between 01:45 and 02:45, IBs started eighteen small fires at King George Dock, not affecting railway property.[8]

A bomb 30 yards (27m) from the railway line damaged Stoneferry Junction signal box, which controlled access to Stoneferry Goods station, bringing down telegraph wires.[9]

### 1/2 July 1940
At 17:54 on the 1st of July an HE hit and set on fire a 2.4 million gallon (11 million litres) storage tank at the Anglo-American Oil facility at Salt End, Hedon. By 07:00 on the 2nd it was still on fire, but not in danger of spreading, and staff had drawn off most of the contents.[10]

### 15/16 August 1940
An unknown number of HEs were dropped on Hessle, close to the main LNER marshalling yard for Hull, at 01:55 on the 16th.[11] There was some minor damage to infrastructure at the yard, but repairs were in hand, and train working was not severely impacted.[12]
'Small craters' were reported on a golf course a mile from the Blackburn Aircraft Company's factory at Brough.[13]

### 19/20 August 1940
The Hessle marshalling yard was hit at 01:49 on the 20th, but the three HEs landed to the east, with one failing to explode. A cluster of IBs landed further east.[14]

### 25 August 1940
IBs fell on Alexandra and Victoria Docks around 21:40: all were quickly extinguished before causing significant damage.[15][16]

### 27/28 August 1940
Drypool Goods railway station on Seward Street damaged.[17][18]

**30 August 1940**
At around 02:00 an HE was dropped on the British Industrial Solvents plant at Salt End, damaging a water main and interrupting the supply to the plant for two hours. Boiler fires to be drawn.[19]

**18/19 September 1940**
At 01:20 on the 19th a cluster of Incendiaries and five HEs were dropped adjacent to the Priory Yard railway sidings, Hessle.[20]

**13 October 1940**
Minor damage to the Wray, Sanderson & Co. Ltd oil mills in Morley Street, production unaffected. Minor damage to gas and water mains and sewers in the vicinity of the British Gas Light Company Ltd gasworks, again not affecting production.[21]

**1 November 1940**
At 06:52 multiple HEs landed close to King George Dock, starting a fire in the timber yard that was quickly extinguished.[22] [23] [24] Some landed in the vicinity of Marfleet railway station, damaging the signal box and blocking the line, although this was quickly cleared and traffic resumed.[25]

**10/11 November 1940**
Between 00:30 and 02:20 on the 11th the railway line between Marfleet and Hedon Racecourse stations was fouled by a barrage balloon cable, which also brought down telephone and block telegraph cables. It was removed by the barrage balloon crew, causing only slight delays.[26]

**12 December 1940**
At 06:14 a fire at British Oil & Cake Mills Ltd on Foster Street caused negligible damage, including to bags of rice stock. On the other side of the River Hull, an IB partly penetrated a gas holder at the British Gas Light Company Ltd's plant, but the holder partly sealed itself. Other bombs landed among the oxide plant, but production was not affected.[27] At the same time there was some damage to the office and yard of the Major & Co. Ltd oil farm in Sculcoates.[28]

**4/5 February 1941**
Single HE on LNER property at 23:00 on the 4th brought down telephone and block telegraph cables in Ella Street; railway traffic between Alexandra Dock and Spring Bank North working at caution. The cable damage was repaired by 11:00 on the 5th.[29] [30]

**14/15 February 1941**
At 22:55 on the 14th two HEs caused minor damage to the Co-Operative Wholesale Society (CWS) Wilmington Flour Mill, with production unaffected. The British Oxygen Co. Ltd plant on Main Street was also damaged.[31] It was later confirmed that although the roof and walls were damaged, there was little damage to production machinery. At the time the plant was being held in reserve, pending the need for increased production.[32]

**16 February 1941**
At 02:10 an HE cratered and damaged 30 yards (27m) of railway siding at the north-east corner of E Block at King George Dock.[33] [34]

**22 February 1941**
At 21:00 there was damage to a railway embankment, and the main passenger and goods line to the docks closed due to a UXB.[35]

An HE between Albert Dock Exchange Sidings and Spring Bank South signal box destroyed both goods lines, leaving a 60ft (18m) crater, into which a light locomotive fell, but causing no casualties.[36] Single line operation was restored on the 28th, although the locomotive had not yet been removed.[37]

A UXB at the Chalk Lane Sidings diverted traffic between Anlaby Road and Hessle Road via the Cottingham South branch line. The Hull-New Holland ferry was suspended due to a suspected unexploded mine (UXM) in the Humber.[38]

### 25/26 February 1941
At 21:00 on the 25th an HE damaged signal lights near Broomfleet station.[39]

### 4 March 1941
British Oil & Cake Mills Ltd's Eagle Mills temporarily closed due to the discovery of a UXB.[40]

### 13 March 1941
At 01:15, a UXB reported on the embankment in the vicinity of the Northgate level crossing near Cottingham station.[41] [42]

### 13/14 March 1941
Extensive railway damage after an HE hit the end of the platform at Wilmington station, damaging the Down line and leaving single-line working on the Up.[43] Normal working recommences from 16:10 on the 14th.[44]

Single-line working was between Sculcoates and Burleigh Street due to a crater between Sculcoates and Hull Bridge.[45] Normal working from 11:30 on the 14th[46] A small crater and a UXB under the turntable reported at Botanic Goods station. Also hit was the former Cannon Street station at 22:56 on the 13th.[47]

At 23:30, HEs and IBs struck the British Oxygen Co. Ltd's plant on Lime Street, causing slight damage to the roof glazing of the fitting shop and stores.[48]

At 00:45 on the 14th four HEs on the south side of Albert Dock blew out three goods lines leading to the riverside quay. There was slight damage to a coal store by a single HE at William Wright Docks,[49] while an UXM landing on the Alexandra Dock branch line leading to the River pier[50] caused the suspension of working to four quays between 07:00 and 10:00 on the 14th.[51]

The New Holland ferry was suspended until further notice due to suspected UXMs in the Humber.[52]

Four HEs hit Wray, Sanderson & Co. Ltd's oil hydrogenation plant, gutting a large warehouse and damaging solvent carrying pipes, holding up production for an estimated two to three weeks.[53] Rose, Downs & Thompson Ltd's Old Foundry on Cannon Street was hit, damaging the walls and roof of the boiler and plating shop.[54]

The same raid also damaged a water reservoir in the area – emptied pending a report by the Regional Engineer. Around twenty mainly small mains were broken, along with one of 18 inches (46cm) and one of 25 inches (64cm). Standpipes and water bowsers were supplying all users, although there remained a risk from UXBs.[55] [56]

### 14/15 March 1941
Another raid caused further damage to water infrastructure. It was later reported that over the two nights around twenty-eight mains had been broken, although it was expected that all would be repaired by the evening of the 17th. In addition to one bomb exploding on the embankment of the covered Keldgate Reservoir, west of Cottingham, another went through the roof, but did not detonate. The reservoir was emptied and the bomb removed, after which it was determined that one roof bay and some supporting columns needed rebuilding.

A number of other UXBs landed near Cottingham Pumping Station, but all but one had been removed. There was minor damage to the Central Waterworks Depot on Clough Road.[57][58]

## 16/17 March 1941

During the night a UXM was found at St Andrew's Dock. At 10:15 on the 18th it was destroyed in a controlled explosion by Royal Navy personnel, causing damage to the north side of the dock wall and some sheds.[59]

## 18/19 March 1941

An HE wrecked the retort house at the British Gas Light Company Ltd's plant. As a result the gas supply to the west side of the city – as far as Cottingham and Dunswell – had to be shut down.[60][61] It was later reported on the 25th that damage was not as serious as first thought, and that supplies to affected areas would be restored in a few days.[62]

There was some superficial damage to Dunswell Pumping Station, not affecting the water supply,[63] although four or five mains larger than 21 inches (53cm) were thought broken, and a number of smaller ones. Damage to sewers was not thought serious.[64] It was eventually determined that thirty-one water mains had been broken, five of 18ft or larger.[65]

Rose, Downs & Thompson Ltd's Old Foundry was damaged again.[66] Premier Oil Extracting Mills in Stoneferry was also hit, with the cattle food stores destroyed, but production unaffected.[67] The boiler house of the CWS Wilmington Flour Mills was also damaged – production expected to be stopped for six to eight weeks.[68]

Another repeat target was the Major & Co. Ltd oil farm in Sculcoates, with an HE demolishing an office, and causing other minor fire damage.[69]

There was damage to electricity infrastructure at 02:53 on the 19th. Some Central Electricity Board lines were damaged between Hull and York, separating Hull from the National Grid, but local supplies were maintaining the load. Within the city some local feeders were damaged.[70]

The line was damaged at Stepney station, stopping services to Withernsea and Hornsea; replacement bus service arranged,[71] with a limited rail service from the 21st,[72] and normal working from 14:00 on 10 April.[73] Other damage stopped services between Driffield and Beverley, and Hull to Scarborough via Bridlington.[74] The track between Beverley Road and Cannon Street station was cratered, and a platelayer injured.[75]

The Alexandra Dock branch was damaged near Chanterlands Avenue Bridge, while the line and road access to Victoria Dock was damaged on South bridge Road.[76] The latter was reopened two days later.[77]

## 21/22 March 1941

The Humber Ferry, suspended since the 13th, resumed at 13:30, but the Admiralty requested a further suspension from 19:00 to 13:30 on the 22nd.[78]

## 31 March/1 April 1941

The roof of ship repairers Stewart & Craig Ltd at 355 Hedon Road was damaged, as was that of shipbuilders and repairers Amos & Smith Ltd's Albert Dock Works on Neptune Street.[79] Rose, Downs & Thompson Ltd's Old Foundry suffered similar damage.[80]

A PM caused minor damage at Victoria Dock, and HEs landed in the vicinity of Albert Dock.[81] A UXM suspended traffic working on the north side of Albert Dock.[82]

A UXM near North Road at 22:45 closed the Hull to Barnsley line between Exchange Siding and Spring Bank South.[83] A PM at the Priory Sidings between 21:00 and 24:00 caused some interference in the marshalling yard.[84]

## 7/8 April 1941

A UXB at Spring Bank West closed the Hull to Bridlington line on the 8th at 00:38.[85] There was thought to be damage to city water mains,[86] but upon further investigation it was found that only one 6-inch main (15cm) was involved.[87]

## 15/16 April 1941

At 03:42 on the 16th a PM badly damaged Stewart & Craig Ltd, while an HE caused slight damage to nearby shipbuilders Brigham & Cowan Ltd.[88] Another PM wrecked the No. 22 Shed at Alexandra Dock Goods station, damaged the dock wall[89] and power cables, and sank a lighter.[90] A UXM fell near No. 32 Shed and all movement in the Dock was suspended on Admiralty instructions.[91] Normal working recommenced from 13:00 on the 17th.[92]

There was blast damage to roofs at the British Oil & Cake Mills Ltd's Eagle Mill, stopping production.[93] A gasholder at the British Gas Light Company Ltd was also damaged, but fully repaired within the following ten days.[94]

## 3/4 May 1941

A PM fell on Alexandra Dock, starting a fire at No. 31 Shed.[95]

## 5/6 May 1941

At 23:42 on the 5th two HEs landed in the vicinity of the Salt End oil farm.[96] HEs at King George Dock damaged No. 3 Shed and a water main, which flooded a grain silo.[97] Railway track between the Dock and Salt End was also damaged.[98]

## 7/8 May 1941

Extensive HE and fire damage to King George and Alexandra Docks.[99] [100] The East Hull Gas Company's premises on St Mark's Street was damaged by fire caused by HEs.[101] J. Rank Ltd's Clarence flour mills were gutted by fire.[102]

Damage was also reported at the British Gas Light Company Ltd, Priestman Brothers Ltd's Holderness Foundry on Thomas Street, the Premier Oil Extracting Company Ltd at Stoneferry, Stewart & Craig Ltd, and British Industrial Solvents Ltd at Salt End.[103] There was superficial damage due to a near miss by a PM to the British Oxygen Company Ltd plant at Lime Street,[104] and roof and window damage at Rose, Downs & Thompson Ltd's Old Foundry.[105]

The raid caused extensive damage to water supply infrastructure in the city, although not as much as initially feared. Supply was sufficient to meet fire-fighting needs, although thirteen mains were damaged, one of 18 inches and the rest no larger than 9 inches. One portable pumping set was in operation, which in addition to the permanent ones was meeting three times normal demand. Four sewers were thought to be damaged.[106]

Outside the eastern city boundary, a UXM in a field 80 yards (73m) north of the track resulted in trains stopping at Hedon station.[107]

## 8/9 May 1941

All damage to railway lines within the city boundary from the previous night's raid were repaired on the 8th, with the exception of the goods line to the Docks.[108] To the west of the city boundary, a single HE cratered the track near Anlaby station at 01:00 on the 9th.[109]

At 03:00 a PM resulted in the burning out of the British Oil & Cake Mills Ltd's Eagle Mill, including the silo. There was superficial damage to Spillers Ltd's Swan Mills, with production unaffected. Stewart & Craig Ltd suffered further blast damage, while the boiler shop of Brigham & Cowan was also damaged.[110] By 12 June repairs at BOCM were progressing, and the plant was partially operational. Full production at Brigham & Cowan had also resumed, but repairs to furnaces were expected to take longer.[111]

Amos & Smith's Naval Stores at William Wright Dock were gutted by fire, the fitting-out shed at Princes Dock wrecked, and the company premises on English Street superficially damaged but still working. The engine shop of the Drypool Dock & Engineering Company Ltd at No. 1 High Street was partially destroyed by fire.[112]

There was further damage to the city water supply on top of that caused previously. Some small areas were being supplied by standpipes and mobile tanks, and the pumping level at Cottingham was 45ft (14m) below normal. Fire services were urged to rely on static supplied where possible. There were a further nineteen mains damaged, including one of 24 inches (61cm) and two of 12 inches (30cm). The amount of chlorine added to the supply was increased. Damage to the sewer system was unclear, although the eastern pumping station was temporarily stopped due to a lack of water supply for the steam plant.[113]

A number of IBs hit the Shell-Mex and BP oil farm at Salt End. Two burned through the roof of Tank 92, igniting petrol vapour, although this was quickly extinguished. Another IB landed on the roof of Tank 36, but did not burn through, while another pierced the roof of Pumphouse B. A subsequent inspection revealed holes in the roofs of Tanks 16, 21 and 36.[114]

### 12 May 1941
At 01:15 three HEs damaged lighters at Princes Dock.[115] Another HE at 02:15 caused no damage.[116]

Three more water mains were damaged, bringing the known total since the night of 7/8 May to seventy-eight. By 16 May all damaged mains had been capped and repairs in hand, with overall supply being maintained by alternative sources, including three water carts and nine standpipes. Use of emergency pumps had stopped on the 9th, and labour and resources for repairs were thought to be sufficient. The main 6ft western outfall, three large sewers and a number of small sewers were damaged. The extensive tank sewer system was kept as full as possible for fire-fighting purposes, although this carried a risk of flooding in the event of heavy rainfall.[117]

### 29 May 1941
Two HEs at 01:57 caused slight damage to railway lines at St Andrew's Dock.[118]

### 29 June 1941
At 01:45 a single HE damaged the quay between Alexandra and King George Docks, while two more at the latter damaged railway track, derailing and damaging a wagon.[119]

### 11 July 1941
During the early hours the railway crossing at Victoria Dock was blocked with debris.[120] Fires were started at the Paragon station permanent way yard, while a PM damaged the English Street Goods Depot.[121] There was also railway damage in the vicinity of Stepney station, interrupting services, but these resumed later that day. A UXB was reported in the Sculcoates Goods Yard.[122]

Eleven HEs struck the recreation ground at Bankside, close to the British Gas Light Company Ltd, but causing no damage.[123] The raid did, however, damage two 25 inch (64cm) water mains.[124]

### 17/18 July 1941
At 01:20 on the 18th the main trunk telephone exchange at the General Post Office was evacuated due to an HE.[125]

Both Southcoates station and the Wilmington signal box were damaged, with the lines blocked between Wilmington Junction and Hornsea sidings, and between Craven Street Bridge and Marfleet Bridge, all due to HEs.[126] Normal services to Hornsea had resumed by 20 July.[127]

During the night, fires were reported at Spillers Ltd's Swan Mill, the East Hull Gas Company and the British Gas Light Company Ltd at Bankside. There was also damage reported at Railway Dock.[128] It was later confirmed that Spillers had been completely gutted.[129]

There was damage to brickwork and the roof of the grab shop at shipbuilders Priestman Brothers Ltd's Holderness Foundry on Thomas Street, while a direct HE hit at Wray, Sanderson & Co. Ltd put the refinery out of action. The roof was damaged at the Premier Oil Extracting Mills Ltd at Stoneferry.[130]

An HE at the Dunswell pumping station severed the 25-inch main.[131] Within the city ten large and thirteen smaller water mains were damaged, with eight mobile tanks and six standpipes in operation.[132] There were at least ten damage incidents involving sewers, and rainfall had caused flooding at Hedon Road Bridge due to the overflow of tank sewers, as previously feared.[133] Repair crews were sent from Sheffield, Doncaster and York, with additional equipment sent from Sheffield, Doncaster and Rotherham.[134]

## 23 July 1941

During the early hours three PMs landed in Alexandra Dock, but did not explode. One detonated at 08:05, sinking three motor lighters, but not damaging the dock itself.[135]

## 21 September 1941

Four HEs – one unexploded – landed on Priory Yard Sidings at 01:35. Bomb crater and slight damage to track in Nos 3 & 4 Sections of the marshalling yard.[136]

## 12/13 October 1941

Damage to No. 1 Shed at Humber Dock from an HE in adjacent street. HE on south-east corner of Railway Dock, damaging dock wall. HE in water at west end of dock damaged wall and lighters. Working unaffected.[137]

## 1 May 1942

Two HEs in the Spring Bank area blocked the Hornsea and Withernsea railway lines with debris.[138] One HE 25 yards (23m) from the Botanical Gardens signal box at 03:30 slewed tracks and brought down telephone and telegraph wires. Normal working (bar the goods Down line) recommenced from 07:30.[139]

## 19/20 May 1942

At 00:15 on the 20th all railway lines under the Craven Street bridge were blocked by HEs,[140] while around fifty HEs and numerous IBs scored direct hits on Alexandra, Victoria and King George Docks.[141] At Alexandra Dock the GPO and LNER telephone lines were cut, and the electricity supply failed. The dock was closed for UXB clearance, but reopened on the 21st. Most of the IBs fell on Victoria Dock, causing a severe fire, which was only brought under control on the 23rd. At King George Dock an HE caused slight damage to No. 14 Warehouse, with dock traffic stopped due to a UXB.[142]

Outside the city, three HEs broke windows at Blackburn Aircraft Ltd at Brough at 00:12,[143] while at 00:19 four HEs hit the RAF station at Hedon, setting a building and an ammunition dump on fire, although this was under control by 01:27.[144]

## 1 August 1942

HEs in the vicinity of the eastern docks from 02:45. One HE at Alexandra Dock caused no significant damage, while one fell in the Timber Yard, and another in Fealby's Yard, causing railway track damage. Two more landed between King George Dock and Salt End at 03:01.[145] [146] [147]

**24 October 1942**
HE on the Permanent Way Department's plumbers' shop at Paragon station at 21:23. Services suspended between 21:50 and 22:50.[148]

**20 December 1942**
HE damage to a railway embankment in the centre of the city at 19:48.[149]

**3 February 1943**
An HE hit the Wray, Sanderson & Co. Ltd seed oil mill around 20:33, damaging windows and blackout precautions. Works stopped.[150]

**5 February 1943**
At 21:15 a barrage balloon fouled telephone, signalling and electrical wires at Alexandra Pier. Trains worked at caution between Spring Bank North and Alexandra Dock. Normal working recommenced at 23:10.[151]

**9 March 1943**
Two HEs hit the Blackburn Aircraft Ltd factory at Brough at 21:20, damaging windows, walls and oil tanks in the boiler house, and partially cutting the electricity supply. Blackout precautions were also damaged.[152]

**24 June 1943**
Between 02:35 and 03:15 an HE destroyed a store at Rose, Downs & Thompson Ltd's Old Foundry. At the same time a Phosphorous Bomb damaged the machine shop at J. Rank Ltd's Clarence Mills.[153]

IBs caused damage to the north-east corner of the roof of Paragon station. All railway company telephones out of action. Several railway wagons burnt out at Victoria Dock. HE at Bridges Junction, between Alexandra Dock and Spring Bank, damaged both Up and Down lines, affecting working to and from Alexandra and King George Docks.[154] Down line clear at 09:10 on the 24th, Up line clear and normal working recommenced from 12:45.[155] All railway telephones fixed by 06:00 on the 25th.[156]

**13/14 July 1943**
Fire reported at the Metal Box Company Ltd on Southcoates Lane. An Oil Bomb started a fire at Victoria Dock, whilst IBs started another at a shed at Alexandra Dock. There were two UXBs at King George Dock, and three more at Alexandra Dock.[157] A HE landed on a signal box at Alexandra Dock, where IBs set fire to a wagon.[158]

Between 01:21 and 02:10 on the 14th a mixture of IBs and HEs hit the Priory Yard Sidings. Bridge carrying Southcoates Lane over railway badly damaged. Hull to Withernsea and goods line to Docks blocked. Signal box also demolished.[159] [160] Line between West Parade Junction and Paragon station temporarily blocked by debris.[161]

Slight blast damage at Stewart & Craig Ltd – production unaffected.[162]

**14/15 March 1944**
Railway wagon damaged by fire at Alexandra Dock.[163] A case of smoke bombs caught fire and exploded in a wagon (LNE 609470) in No. 23 Shed at 21:30 on the 14th. Two railway staff were hospitalised locally, while an American soldier was treated by US authorities. At 01:00 on the 15th a fire was reported on a freighter in the Dock, caused by smoke bombs falling from the crane tray while being loaded. Extinguished by 01:48, with no injuries or serious damage.[164]

# Chapter 7
# *Tabula Rasa*

Following the devastation of the heavy raids in May and July 1941, in early 1942 the Hull Corporation commissioned the eminent town planner Professor Patrick Abercrombie to produce a post-war rebuilding scheme. Abercrombie was already working on similar plans for both the County of London and Greater London (published in 1943 and 1944, respectively), so for the Hull project he was assisted by the architect Sir Edwin Lutyens. The city, it was hoped, would benefit from a clean slate thanks to both the destruction by the Luftwaffe and the slum clearances that had been in progress before the war. The result of the work was published in 1946 as *A Plan for the City & County of Kingston upon Hull*.[1]

Abercrombie and Lutyens' proposals were nothing if not ambitious, recommending that the centre of the city be significantly redesigned, including the creation of a more centralised retail district at the western end of Queen's Gardens, a theatre and cultural quarter to the north, and beyond it a new main rail terminus to replace Paragon station.[2]

Building on pre-war experience, residential expansion would be largely restricted to the edges of the city, but also a 'satellite' development at Burton Constable, predicated on improved road and rail access to Hull. Within the city, although the railways in general were to be retained, it was noted that the number of level crossings on the low-level lines were

The post-war replacement Cecil Cinema on the corner of Ferensway and Anlaby Road.

A long way from home: the PS *Tattershall Castle* in retirement as a hospitality venue on the River Thames. (Courtesy of Nick Cooper)

a serious impediment to road traffic, and so should be raised. A large 'Youth and Sports' complex would be built north of Sutton Road, on the east side of the River Hull.

Many of the industries on the banks of the River Hull were to be moved to the east side, principally around Drypool, leaving the river lined by warehouses only. Even more radical was the idea that the river's course through the city could be straightened out by a series of diversions omitting the more prominent meanders.[3] The fishing industry was to be relocated from the western docks to Salt End.

The *Plan* also revived the proposal of a Humber Bridge from Hessle to Barton-upon-Humber on the North Lincolnshire coast that had been submitted to Parliament in the early 1930s, but later abandoned. A suspension bridge with a span of 4,500ft (1,370m) was suggested, acknowledging that that would make it the longest in the world.[4]

Ultimately very little of the *Plan* came to fruition. Hull suffered severely from a post-war decline, and Abercrombie and Lutyens' proposals were simply unaffordable. At the end of the 1950s, while still selling off the surplus stock of the *Plan*, the Corporation inserted an apologetic note from the Town Planner explaining why so little of it had happened. Much post-war rebuilding was haphazard and utilitarian, with little consideration for how it would fare in the decades to follow.

The Beeching Axe fell on some but not all of Hull's railway lines. The branches to Hornsea and Withernsea were closed, severely restricting the future development prospects of both destinations, as well as all the stations served in between. The paddle steamers *Tattershall Castle* and *Wingfield Castle* were retired in the mid-1970s, leaving the *Lincoln Castle* to

Schoolboys play precariously in the abandoned city centre docks in 1980. (Courtesy of Nick Cooper)

The same view in 2009, with the docks repurposed as the Hull Marina. (Courtesy of Nick Cooper)

The Deep aquarium on the site of the former Citadel. (Courtesy of Nick Cooper)

battle on until it was replaced by the ex-Isle of Wight diesel paddler *Farringford* in 1978. The *Wingfield Castle* is appropriately preserved in Hartlepool, where she was built, while the *Tattershall Castle* is a popular hospitality venue on the River Thames. The *Lincoln Castle* was controversially scrapped in 2010, when the final owner refused to sell her for preservation.

The city-centre docks were abandoned and lay derelict for decades until Humber and Railway Docks were successfully re-opened as the Hull Marina in 1983, and the Prince's Quay shopping centre was partly built over Princes Dock, opening in 1991. Time will tell what will happen to the now derelict western docks. The site of the former Citadel is now occupied by popular tourist attraction The Deep, the world's only 'submarium', housing thousands of sea creatures in 2.5 million litres (550,000 gallons) of water; its striking architecture evoking the earlier fortification.

Hull still bears the scars of the Second World War, if one pauses to look. A residential terrace disrupted here, a truncated building there, and the shell of the former National Cinema on Beverley Road standing as a gaunt symbol of the city's sacrifice. At Cherry Cobb Sands, the docks decoy survives, and in a 2003 television programme was shown to still 'work' half a century on.[5]

In 2017, Hull celebrates its status as the UK City of Culture, and faces the future as it always has, with quiet resolution and an intense but modest local pride.

*Unbowed*
*Unbroken*
*Undefeated*

*We are Hull*

The memorial to civilian casualties in the Western Cemetery on Chanterlands Avenue. (Courtesy of Barnaby Cooper)

# Appendix 1

# Fatalities in Hull Due to War Operations

The total number of named deaths due to War Operations in Hull recorded by the Commonwealth War Graves Commission (CWGC) numbers 1,171. This includes fifteen members of the armed services, and five of the Merchant Navy (four as civilian deaths, one as a service death). This contrasts with the fatalities tabulated in *A North East Coast Town* – based on Corporation and ARP records – totalling 1,066 and 1,016 seriously injured. The wartime population of Hull was around 320,000.

There may be some unidentified fatalities, although of some 19,000 deaths registered in Hull between the June quarters of 1940 and 1945, only six have no known name. Two are two females, five males, and two indeterminate, and three are aged zero, one being a known air raid casualty. In contrast there are no civilians in CWGC's records who cannot be reconciled with a death registration, either in Hull (1,148), Holderness (13), or elsewhere (8).

Known deaths are listed below by date of air raid or other fatal event, by place of death or injury, and alphabetically by surname, with exceptions for family members with a different surname. Married couples are indicated as "husband" and "wife" in descending age order, and children indented as "son" or "daughter." Exceptions are where only one parent died, in which case the indication is "father" or "mother" to co-listed children. Where only siblings died, they are indicated as appropriate.

Abbreviations used:
AFS = Auxiliary Fire Service
ARI = Anlaby Road Institution [188 Anlaby Road][1]
ARW = Air Raid Warden
BHB = Base Hospital, Beverley [Westwood Hospital]
BHC = Base Hospital, Cottingham [City Hospital/Castle Hill Hospital]
BRI = Beverley Road Institution [160 Beverley Road][2]
FAP = First Aid Post
HCP = Hull City Police
HRH = Hedon Road Hospital [Hull Maternity Hospital][3]
HRI = Hull Royal Infirmary [Prospect Street]
LNER = London & North Easter Railway
NFS = National Fire Service
RISB = [Hull] Royal Infirmary (Sutton Branch)
VHSC = Victoria Hospital for Sick Children

## 25 August 1940
Bolton, Betty (sister, 15)
   Bolton, Doreen (sister, 6)
Scott, Frederick (husband, 25)
   Scott, Dorothy Amelia (wife, 22)
Smith, William L'Estrange Cromer (34)
Wade, Cyril Ernest (35)

## 27/28 August 1940
Haughton, John William (85) – injured, died at HRI

## 13 October 1940
Hairsine, Marion (22)
Walker, Doreen (17) – injured, died at RISB

## 22 October 1940
Brown, Dorothy (28) – injured, died at BRI
Freeman, Ivy (30)

## 1 November 1940
Trotter, Max Frank – AFS Fireman (28) – assumed injured,[4] died 04 November 1940 at BRI

## 4/5 February 1941
Bayram, George (husband, 60)
   Bayram, Margaret Ann (wife, 60) – injured, died at BRI
Dexter, Jack (40)
Hoggard, Cyril Theodore Day (44)

**14/15 February 1941**
Ramm, William Herbert (18) – assumed injured,
died 23 March 1941 at BRI

**22 February 1941**
Buttle, Dalton (39)
Hinchliffe, William Henry – Firewatcher (46)
Oxley, Robert Lacey (husband, 55)
Oxley, Violet (wife, 53)

**23/24 February 1941**
Adamson, Frederick (66) - injured, died 09
November 1946[5]
Anderton, Edith (34)
Bridger, Ida (mother, 25) - assumed injured, died
at ARI
Bridger, Patricia (son, 13 months) - assumed
injured, died at ARI
Crawford, Florence Walker (54)
Havercroft, Joseph William (67)
Jordan, Lena (56)
Mills, Ernest Albert (75)
Perkins, Selina (mother, 68)
    Perkins, Edith Selina - ARW (daughter, 40)
Proby, Sarah Elizabeth (73)
Richardson, Albert Edward (husband, 44)
    Richardson, Minnie (wife, 40)

**25/26 February 1941**
Walker, Isaac (51)

**1 March 1941**
Govier, John (husband, 53)
    Govier, Annie May (wife, 52) – injured, died
    02 March 1941 at BRI
Pollard, John Edward (husband, 64)
    Pollard, Sarah Elizabeth (wife, 63)
Williamson, Arthur (53)

**8 March 1941**
Florence, George Kenneth (25)[6]

**13/14 March 1941**
Addey, Annie (47)
Blenkinsop, Joseph William (54)
Cooper, Harold Matthew, A.I.C. - Assistant Gas
Identification Officer (25) - injured, died 15
March 1941 at BRI
Davies, Frederick - Police Fireman, HCP (28)
Foster, George (79)
Freeman, John (17 months)
Gaskell, Neville Seller - Firewatcher (27)
Green, Trevor (3)
Hare, George (31)
Hewitt, Will - Police Fireman, HCP (29)
Hopper, Annie (71)

Johnson, William Henry (74)
Miller, Margaret (7)
Neesom, Ralph Ernest - ARW (father, 38)
    Neesom, Stuart Gordon (son, 6)
Nelson, Elizabeth Jane (mother, 53)
    Nelson, Elsie (daughter, 21)
    Nelson, Thomas Albert (son, 13)
Nicholson, Walter (41)
Owens, Harry Thurlow (12, brother)
    Owens, Doreen (sister, 3)
    Owens, David (brother, 9 months)
Page, Albert William (57)
Quest, Emily (62)
Rasmussen, Jens Laurits (57) - assumed injured,
died 15 March 1941 at BRI
Richardson, Walter Straker - Police Fireman,
HCP (36)
Sanders, Clara Ann (72)
    Sanders, Salisbury (7)
Senior, Eva - WVS (63)
Shipley, William (52)
Southwick, Maria (wife, 60)
    Southwick, Charles (husband, 55)
Spencer, Robert (8)
Staveley, Bernard James (husband, 24)
    Staveley, Joan Marguerite (wife, 22)
Taylor, Peter (12 months)
Trowill, William Gibson (81) - injured, died
at BRI
Waslin, Emily (73)
Wheldale, Harold (4)
Wilson, Walter - ARW (56)
Woodhead, George William (45) - injured, died
20 July 1945 at BRI

**14/15 March 1941**
Dobson, Mary (60)
Gardham, Marie Auguste Sophie (88)
Garside, Thomas (husband, 53)
    Garside, Florence Ida (wife, 45)
Marshall, Dora (62)
Marsay, Mary Thornton (62)
Moore, Frederick (husband, 38)
    Moore, Edith (wife, 30)
    Moore, George (son, 6)
    Moore, Donald (son, 3)
Norris, Ann (mother, 45)
    Norris, Marion (daughter, 8)
Rawlings, George William (45) – injured, died 26
May 1943 at Hull Naval Hospital
Robinson, Bertie (65)
Shaw, Lillian (52)
Stansfield, Herbert Percy (42)
Stockdale, George (husband, 74)
    Stockdale, Alice (wife, 70)

## 18/19 March 1941

Barratt, Selina (58)
Beckett, Kate (48)
Bentley, Albert Arthur (38)
Burnett, George Henry (54) – injured, died 12 May 1941 at Seacroft Hospital, Leeds
Cox, Thomas – Home Guard (father, 49)
   Cox, Dorothy (daughter, 8)
   Cox, Geoffrey (son, 8)
Dalton, Laura Ethel (sister, 14)
   Dalton, Barbara (sister, 11)
   Dalton, Mavis May (sister, 6)
Dixon, Phyllis (sister-in-law,[7] 21)
Faulkner, May Evelyn (sister-in-law, 32)
Farnsworth, Kate Ena (36)
   Farnsworth, Eric William Gilbert (6)
Fulstow, Minnie (wife, 75)
   Fulstow, Robert Bryan (husband, 74)
Gladstone, Ellen (mother, 33
   Gladstone, Joan (daughter, 11)
   Gladstone, Jack (son, 7)
   Gladstone, Walter (son, 4)
   Gladstone, Shirley (daughter, 23 months)
Gow, Francis John (50)
Gregory, Frederick Russell (57)
Griffin, Thomas (husband, 70)
   Griffin, Mary Hannah (wife, 68)
Guest, Frederick Colin (52)
Hale, Ada (55)
Hargrave, Ernest William (husband, 50)
   Hargrave, Mary Jane (wife, 48)
   Hargrave, Doris (daughter, 19)
   Hargrave, Ernest William (son, 15)
   Hargrave, Stephen (son, 13)
   Hargrave, Jean (daughter, 11)
Harrison, Henry (43)
Hopkinson, Walter (step-father, 38) – injured, died at Hedon Road FAP
Ironside, Irene Stewart – ARP Telephonist (29)
Jordan, James Albert (33) – assumed injured, died at HRI
Kay, Gladys (mother, 26)
Kay, Joyce (daughter, 3)
Kendall, Florence (mother, 37)
   Kendall, Florence Mary (daughter, 15)
   Kendall, David William (son, 14)
   Kendall, Terence Brian (son, 11)
   Kendall, Irene Isabel (daughter, 9)
   Kendall, Kathleen Dawn (daughter, 7)
   Kendall, Iris Brenda (daughter, 4)
King, Norah (mother, 37)
   King, Frank (son, 34)
   King, Betty (daughter, 3)
Kirby, Fred (69)
Lamb, Barbara (13)
Lissiter, Frederick William – Firewatcher (61)

Loft, Horace (36)
Lyell, George William (19)
Rea, Doreen (step-daughter, 16) – injured, died 24 McCune, Walter Alfred (42)
March 1941 at HRHl
Mulchinock, Ethel (mother, 51) – injured, died at HRH
   Mulchinock, Ethel Mary (daughter, 28) – injured, died at Hedon Road FAP
Ness, Kathleen (sister, 30)
   Ness, Eileen (sister, 21)
Nicholson, Frederick (55)
Pearce, Arthur (70)
Poole, Hannah (née Cockerill, 45)
   Cockerill, Florence (daughter, 18)
   Cockerill, Winifred (daughter, 14)
Porter, Margaret (mother, 32)
   Porter, Margaret (daughter, 10)
   Porter, Jean (daughter, 6)
   Porter, Larry (son, 3)
   Porter, Dennis (son, 22 months)
Proctor, Rose (mother, 31)
   Proctor, Charles Neil (son, 5)
   Proctor, Valerie Ann (daughter, 18 months)
Roberts, Alfred (43) – died at HRI
Roberts, Ella (mother, 37)
   Roberts, Albert Edward (daughter, 8)
Scales, Ellen Veronica (husband, 59)
   Scales, Albert George (wife, 56)
Scott, George William (husband, 39)
   Scott, Minnie Zeddi (wife, 33)
   Scott, Margaret Rosalind (daughter, 7)
   Scott, Douglas (son, 5)
   Scott, Valerie (daughter, 4)
   Scott, Doreen (daughter, 23 months)
Setterfield, Frederick William – Firewatcher (60)
Shaw, Albert Leonard – ARW (40)
Shaw, Edith (26)
Thickett, Thomas (husband, 52)
   Thickett, Alice May (wife, 48)
   Thickett, Arthur (son, 17)
Tozer, Gertrude (mother, 25)
   Tozer, Frederick Dennis (son, 4)
Warden, Florence Ada (32) – assumed injured, died 13 April 1941 at BRI
Wilkins, Marion (sister, 26)
Wilkinson, Walter (48)
Wisher, Ellen (64)

## 1 March/1 April 1941

Allsopp, James Harold – Driver, Army Service Corps (28) [8]
Ayrton, Robert Seymour (brother, 17)
   Ayrton, Christine (sister, 15)
   Ayrton, Florence (sister, 12)
Bayston, Phyllis Evelyn (20)

Braithwaite, Lucy – WVS (43)

Brocklebank, Myras (40)

Brook, Eva (48)

Butler, Bramwell – Firewatcher (44)

Carmichael, Andrew (31)

Carrington, Ada Ann (62)

Diamond, David, DPH, MRCP – Deputy Medical Officer of Health (42

Ellis, Ivor Dennis – ARW (22)

Garton, Robert – Constable, HCP (46)

Goltman, Mark (65)

Hendrickson, Sidney Wilfred (42)

Hessell, John William Underwood (32)

Howard, Emma (80)

Jackson, Edgar (46) – injured, died 09 April 1941 at VHSC

Jennison, George Henry (husband, 62)
   Jennison, Annie Elizabeth (wife, 56)

Johnson, Lilian (37)

Jones, William Phillip (husband, 56)
   Jones, Amelia Anne (wife, 54)
   Jones, Daniel William (son, 24)
   Jones, Constance (daughter, 17)
   Jones, Stella (daughter, 12)
   Burgess, Dora (daughter of William and Amelia Jones , 26) – injured, died at BRI

Leng, Leo Sidney – Gunner, 173 Battery, 62 Heavy Anti-Aircraft Regiment, Royal Artillery (29) [9]

Lofthouse, Charles Neville – ARW (50)

Lythe, Reuben Christopher (husband, 52)
   Lythe, Harriett Dorothy (wife, 47) – injured, died 02 April 1941 at BRI

Marshall, Arthur Henry (husband, 67)
   Marshall, Lucy Ann (wife, 66)

Marshall, Henry – Firewatcher (28)

Marsters, Lilian Mabbott – WVS (mother, 43)
   Marsters, Gordon (son, 11)
   Marsters, Bessie (daughter, 8)

Meggitt, Otto Fowler – Aircraftman 2nd Class, RAF Volunteer Reserve (30) [10]

Seward, Frances (87)

Turner, Harold – Deputy Post Leader, Wardens' Service (father, 54) – injured, died at VHSC
   Turner, Denis – ARP Cyclist Messenger (son, 18)

Walker, John Denis (24)

Wood, Susan (mother, 38)
   Wood, Joyce (daughter, 14)
   Wood, Geoffrey (son, 11)
   Wood, Mavis (daughter, 7)

## 3 April 1941

Fullard, Harry – Firewatcher (17) – injured, died at Morrill Street FAP

## 15/16 April 1941

Adamson, Benjamin (husband, 35)
   Adamson, Sarah (wife, 31)
   Adamson, Brian (son, 2)

Acklam, Mary Gwendoline (neé Jordan, mother, 51)
   Jordan, May (daughter, 9)

Batty, Beatrice (16)

Beckett, Elsie (26)

Bowden, Emma (mother, 73)
   Bowden, Gladys Louisa Dashwood (daughter, 34)
   Bowden, Samuel (son, 47)
   Bowden, Ethel (wife of Samuel, 45)
   Bowden, Kenneth (son of Samuel and Ethel, 14)

Boylan, Christiana (wife, 64)
   Boylan, Hugh (husband, 62)

Craker, Polly (aunt, 49)
   Craker, Thomas (nephew, 17)

Danby, William (husband, 49)
   Danby, Lottie Muriel (wife, 48)

Ellerby, Lizzie (64)

Haywood, Mary (63)

Jensen, Fanny (mother, 29)
   Jensen, Philip (son, 4 months)

Longthorn, George Herbert (39)

Longworth, Joseph Samuel (73) – assumed injured, died same day at Morrill Street [FAP]

Lowson, Hilda (26)

Marsden, Frank (40)

Matthews, William (father, 37)
   Matthews, Renee (daughter, 11)

Middleton, Clarence Richard – ARP Instructor (father, 41)
   Middleton, Dennis (son, 15)

Ness, Lucy Ann (70)

Nixon, Tom Henry (72)

Oaten, William Walter (husband, 58)
   Oaten, Margaret Naomi (wife, 57)

Omer, Ada (74)

Orange, Annie Elizabeth (68)

Ounsworth, Annie (wife, 70)
   Ounsworth, George Henry (husband, 69)

Parker, John William (60) – injured, died 01 June 1941 at BHB.

Petch, John William (husband, 48)
   Petch, Clementina (wife, 36)
   Petch, Audrey (daughter, 16)
   Petch, John (son, 2)

Richardson, John (husband, 42)
   Richardson, Elsie (wife, 33)

Sadler, Margaret (38)

Service (father, 27)
   Shaw, Sylvia Brenda (daughter, 5)

Sharpe, Sarah Jane – FAP Member (mother, 38)
   Sharpe, Eileen (daughter, 12)

Sharpe, Olga Miriam (daughter, 11)
    Sharpe, un-named (daughter, <1 day)
Shaw, Charles Richard – ARP Decontamination
Spalding, Dorothy (16)
Tointon, Enid (10)
Walker, Ann Eleanor (sister, 66)
    Walker, Minnie (sister, 61)
Withers, Catherine (61)

## 25 April 1941
Gayer, David Edward (45)
Hammond, Frederick William (father, 42)
    Hammond, Peter (son, 6)
    Hammond, Margaret (daughter, 4)
    Hammond, Colin (son –age 21 months)
    Hammond, Jean Mary (daughter, 6 months)
King, Albert (44)
Thrussell, John Robert (16) – assumed injured, died at same day at ARI

## 5/6 May 1941
Rowe, John (13)

## 7/8 & 8/9 May 1941
As there were two very heavy raids on these consecutive nights, allocating specific deaths appropriately is somewhat imprecise. *ANECT* gives the casualties as follows.

7/8 May 1941: 203 killed, 165 seriously injured
8/9 May 1941: 217 killed, 160 seriously injured

In contrast, CWGC records show the following totals for deaths or ultimately fatal injuries across the three days as:

7 May = 35
8 May = 237
9 May = 120

The 7 May deaths obviously relate to the 7/8 May raid, as the 9 May ones do to 8/9 May raid,[11] but the issue is those dated 8 May, which could be either. This total of 392 also falls short of the *ANECT* total of 420, but includes six service personnel deaths (including probables), and it is entirely possible that there are more, which may well make up the shortfall.

Using a combination of newspaper death notices, classified raid reports, and cross-referencing casualty locations, what follows is an attempt to group the fatalities as best as possible, giving:

7/8 May = 193
8 May = 7
8/9 May = 190

## 7/8 May 1941
Andrew, Ivy Blanche (mother, 38)
    Andrew, Joyce (daughter, 8)
Atkin, Edna (mother, 35)
    Atkin, Harold John (son, 8)
    Atkin, Julian Bryan (son, 2)
Barker, George Edward – LNER Police Constable (65)
Barker, Minnie (mother, 40)
    Barker, Vera (daughter, 20)
Bartle, Joseph Hina (54)
Batchelor, Sarah (73)
Bewick, Edward Edwin (71)
Black, Louis – ARW/Firewatcher (49)
Blakey, Florence (18)
Blenkinsop, Diana (67)
Boase, William Henry (husband, 35)
    Boase, Agnes Rita (wife, 33)
    Boase, Elizabeth Maureen (daughter, 4)
Bolton, Arthur – Divisional Office, Cyclist Messenger Service Corps (41)
Borrill, Jane Isabella – WVS (58)
Bosley, Miranda May (wife, 48)
    Bosley, Walter David (husband, 47)
    Bosley, Arthur John – Gunner, 14 Anti-Tank Regiment, Royal Artillery (son, 20)[12]
    Bosley, Charles William (son, 5)
Bristow, Vincent (husband, 26)
    Bristow, Catherine Christina (wife, 19)
Bush, Elizabeth (husband, 82)
    Bush, John William (wife, 75)
Bushell, Stephen Henry, DSM [13] – Chief Petty Officer, HMS *Pembroke*,[14] Royal Navy (55) [15] [16]
Carmichael, Ernest William (husband,)
    Carmichael, Lily (wife, 58)
Carter, William George (husband, 35)
    Carter, Olive May (wife, 27)
    Carter, Brenda (daughter, 18 months)
Chadwick, Peter Maurice (brother, 5)
    Chadwick, Keith Patrick (brother, 4)
Chambers, William (60)
Charles, Harriet (mother, 44)
    Charles, Harold (son, 16)
    Charles, Stanley (son, 13)
    Charles, Ronald (son, 9)
    Charles, Carol (daughter, 18 months)
Chester, Mary Ellen (63)
    Clark, Joyce Dorothy (21)
Cloury, Eliza Ann (74)
Cooper, Margaret Ellen (mother, 81)
    Cooper, Olive Mercy "Cissie" (daughter, 51)
Cooper, Richard (27)
    Croser, John William (husband, 77)
    Croser, Jane (wife, 75) – injured, died at BRI
Croser, Ida Mary (daughter, 43)
Cullingworth, Henry Cook (48)

Daniels, Harriett (71)
Dawson, Sarah Jane (83)
Denchaw, Ching (63)
Dickens, Joachim Frederick (58)
Dove, Albert Edward (father, 52)
    Davis, Florence (step-daughter,[17] 31) – died 14 May 1941 at VHSC
    Dove, Alice V (daughter, 19) – assumed injured, died 13 May 1941 at BHC
    Dove, Beatrice (daughter, 16)
    Dove, Albert (son, 13)
    Dove, Adelaide (daughter, 11)
    Dove, Ronald (son, 7)
    Dove, Amelia M (daughter, 6)
    Dove, Brian (son, 4)
Dumbleton, Thomas Arthur – Engine Room Artificer 5th Class, HMS *Beaver*,[18] Royal Navy (21)[19]
Eastwood, Muriel (sister, 27)
    Eastwood, Kenneth (brother, 19)
Eccles, George William (62)
Eden, William (60)
Fagan, Thomas – Stoker, HM Trawler Justifier,20 Royal Naval Patrol Service (24)
Fisher, Dora (44)
Flanagan, John (50)
Fox, George William (47)
Freeman, Arthur (69)
Frost, William Ernest (63)
Garbutt, Samuel – Firewatcher (69)
Gardham, James (husband, 51)
    Gardham, Susan (wife, 43)
Gardner, John (husband,)
    Gardner, Olive (wife, 59)
Greenley, William James (father-in-law,)
    Greenley, Amy Gibson (daughter-in-law[21], 27)
    Greenley, William (daughter of Amy, 23 months)
Guy, Annie Elizabeth (78)
    Hailstone, Bertha (mother, 43) – injured, died at RISB
    Hailstone, Joseph Lawrence (son, 16) – injured, died at RISB
    Hailstone, Eric James (son, 3) – injured, died at RISB
Halliday, George "Jack" Henry – ARW (63)
Hanna, Robert Cecil (52)
Hardisty, Cyril (40)
Harrison, Audrey (sister, 10)
    Harrison, Jean (sister, 5)
Haswell, Joyce (mother, 21)
    Haswell, Brenda (daughter, 2)
    Haswell, Joyce (daughter, 6 months)
Heckford, Frederick William (12)
Henderson, Joseph (81)
Hildred, Harold Desmond – Firewatcher (17)
Hill, George Benjamin – Firewatcher (50)

Hill, Mary Joan (22)
Hogan, John (58)
Holt, Herbert (60)
Kelly, John – Firewatcher (55)
Kitching, Jabez (husband, 59)
    Kitching, Lena (wife, 56)
        Kitching, Iris (daughter, 20)
Lammiman, Annie Elizabeth (64)
Lister, Bessie (mother, 27)
    Lister, Robert William (son, 5)
Longthorn, Harry (31)
Lyons, Annie (mother, 46)
    Lyons, George (son, 16)
    Lyons, Joyce (daughter, 13)
    Lyons, Colin (son, 3)
Lyons, Richard (70)
Macmillan, Jean Stephenson (58)
Maguire, Thomas Ernest – ARW (husband, 45)
    Maguire, Matilda Isobel (wife, 43)
    Maguire, Mary Yvonne (daughter, 15)
    Maguire, Therese Madeline (daughter, 12)
Marshall, Hannah (grandmother, 55)
    Marshall, Ivy May (granddaughter[22], 10)
Mays, Herbert (59)
Moody, Mary Elizabeth (grandmother, 60)
    Moody, Dorothea Mary (granddaughter[23], 7)
Moore, Lilian Lucy (husband,)
    Moore, William (wife, 34)
Murray, Samuel (62)
Neville, Frederick William (14)
Nobbs, Jessie (27)
O'Brian, Thomas (husband, 45)
    O'Brian, Florrie (wife, 43)
    O'Brian, Doreen (daughter, 13)
Olsen, Amy (50)
Omer, Cyril – ARW (husband, 41)
    Omer, Lilian – WVS (wife, 32)
Player, Arthur Leonard (65)
Port, Stanley – Aircraftman 1st Class, 942 Balloon Squadron, Royal Air Force [Royal Air Force Volunteer Reserve] (27)[24]
Pratt, William – Home Guard (father, 33)
    Pratt, Hilary "Bunty" Mary Revell (daughter, 4)
Puckering, Louisa – WVS (64)
Raper, Frances Hannah (47)
Rea, Ida Mary (sister, 17)
    Rea, Dennis Herbert (brother, 16)
Rees, Frederick John Stanley (45)
Revell, Ada Maud (mother-in-law, 62)
    Revell, Ida (daughter-in-law,[25] 38)
    Revell, Sylvia (daughter of Ida, 10)
Richardson, Gerald (13)
Ridley, William Henry (father, 45)
    Ridley, Bryan Robert (son, 14)
Robb, Alexander (husband, 78)
    Robb, Mary "Polly" Ann (wife, 56)

Robb, Amy (daughter-in-law[26], 27)
Robb, Eric (daughter of Amy, 2)
Rowe, John (husband, 63)
  Rowe, Annie Elizabeth (wife, 51)
  Rowe, Ellen (daughter, 19)
Sargeant, Leonard John (67)
Schooler, Alexander – Fireman, AFS (42)
Sedgwick, Francis, MA – Vicar of St. Philip's, Hull;
Canon and Prebendary of York Minster (68)
Smith, Frederick (44)
Smith, James (husband, 64)
  Smith, Caroline Isabella (wife, 55)
  Smith, Jessie (daughter, 17)
Smith, Walter (58)
Soulsby, Alice (grandmother[27], 68)
  Soulsby, Eileen May (granddaughter, 14)
  Wilson, Eunice (granddaughter, 5)
  Wilson, Philip Leslie (grandson, 3 weeks)
Stonehouse, Charles Wilson (63)
Taylor, Florence (55)
Tennison, Dorothy Hayton (29)
Tinmouth, Vera (20)
Todd, Thomas (38)
Trushell, Florence (18)
Tummon, Albert (husband, 71)
  Tummon, Agnes (wife, 69)
Walker, John Thomas (68)
Walker, Sidney (51)
Waller, George William – Fireman, AFS (38) –
injured, died at RISB
Wallis, Frederick (54)
  Wallis, Catherine "Kitty" (48)
  Wallis, Frederick Henry (15)
  Wallis, Barbara Jane (11)
Watson, Alan (husband, 39)
  Watson, Jennie (wife, 32)
  Watson, Ronald (son, 6)
Wood, William (69)
Woodbridge, Gertrude Leah (mother, 30)
  Woodbridge, Brian George (son, 5)
  Woodbridge, Colin (son, 11 months)
Woodmansey, Sidney (15)
Woods, John Francis – LNER Police Constable (52)
Wordsworth, Alice Maud (70)

## 8 May 1941 – raid unknown

Adams, George Henry (39)
Baker, Albert Victor Charles (60)
Cook, George – Seaman, Merchant Navy (26)[28]
Fisher, Harold – ARW (32) – injured, died 24
May 1941 at Pinderfields Emergency Hospital,
Wakefield
Fox, Hannah (66)
Pockley, William – American citizen (48)
Revell, Arthur – ARW (60)

## 8/9 May 1941

Abdullah, Qaid (38)
Allen, Tom – Merchant Navy (41)[29]
Allison, Albert Edward (30) – injured, died
10 May 1941 at BHC
Allison, George[30] (64)
Anderson, Amelia (54)
Anderson, Joseph (husband, 73)
  Anderson, Elizabeth (wife, 73) – injured, died
  at Anne Street Almshouses
Andrews, John William – Fireman, AFS (47)
Arton, Leslie Benson, Leading Fireman, AFS (34)
Auld, Lilian (daughter, 12)
Bedford, Jessie (mother, 45)
  Bedford, Frank (son, 20)
  Bedford, Alan (son, 15)
Bedford, Thomas William (husband, 40)
Bedford, Ruby Lilian (wife, 30)
Bell, Florence Eva (32)
Best, Herbert Edward – Police Fireman,
HCP (46)
Bottrill, Norah (35) – injured, died 24 May 1941
at 8 Elm Grove, De La Pole Avenue
Brady, Elsie (mother, 42)
  Brady, William (son, 19)
Branton, Alfred (63)
Brennan, Florence (63)
Brooker, Cyril (husband, 35)
  Brooker, Edith Mary (wife, 33)
  Brooker, Ronald (son, 9)
  Brooker, Marjorie (daughter, 1 month)
Brown, Arthur (father, 58)
  Brown, Elizabeth Mary (daughter, 20)
Brown, Hetty (47)
Brown, Robert Verner – Firewatcher (53)
  Burwood, Charlotte (60)[31]
  Burwood, Violet (daughter 30)
  Burwood, Eunice (daughter of Violet,[32] 3)
Camm, Charlotte (55)
Carter, Jerry George Edward (husband, 57)
  Carter, May (wife, 52)
  Carter, Alice Maud (daughter, 11)
Coates, George Reginald – Home Guard (43)
Collinson, Catherine Mercy (grandmother, 57)
  Collinson, Dorothy (granddaughter, 12)
Cook, John Hopkinson (41) – injured, died 12
August 1941 at Seacroft Hospital, Leeds
Cossey, Henry Arthur (husband, 58)
  Cossey, Laura Mary Ann (wife, 58)
Cottam, George Cyril – Patrol Officer, AFS (31)
Cressey, Leonard Alfred Henry – Fireman,
AFS (48)
Cropper, James Thomas (38)
Cuthbert, Thomas Howard (77) – injured, died
12 May 1941 at BRI
Daley, John William (father, 72)

Dearing, Ernest Henry (43)

Deltour, Louis (husband, 86)
   Deltour, Mabel Isabel – WVS (wife, 43)

Dent, Edith (mother, 37)
   Dent, John (son, 2)
   Dent, Albert (son, 13 months)

Donovan, William (39)

Dowell, John (husband, 69)

Dowell, Eliza Louisa (wife, 60)

Ellerker, William Londesborough (father, 42)
   Ellerker, William Londesborough (son, 10)
   Ellerker, Joan (daughter, 8)

Etherington, Walter Andrew (34)

Farmery, Tom Edrick (67) – injured, died at RISB

Farrow, Gertrude (66)

Fitchett, Thomas (husband, 67)

Fitchett, Mary Jane (wife, 60)
   Fitchett, Mary (daughter-in-law,[33] 23)
   Fitchett, Raymond (son of Mary, 4)
   Fitchett, Maureen (daughter of Mary, 17 months)

Foley, Clifford William Robinson, ARW (33)

Foster, Charles (57)

Foston, James (husband, 76)
   Foston, Mary Jane (wife, 71)
   Foston, Arthur (son, 30)

Fowler, George Cavill – Fireman, AFS (33)[34]

Freer, Florence May (24) – injured, died at BHC

Gallant, Ernest Wellington – Firewatcher (18)

Gibson, Charles Campion (husband, 49)
   Gibson, Ella (wife, 49)

Gibson, George Robert (66)

Goodson, Irene Hardy (mother, 34)
   Goodson, Ernest (son, 10)

Grange, Thomas (64)

Gray, Robert Arthur – FAP Member (33) – injured, died at BRI

Griffiths, Samuel George (60)

Grinsdale, Alfred (61)

Hague, Harold (11)

Hardwidge, Sidney (husband, 36)
   Hardwidge, Elsie Miriam (wife, 35)

Harper, Ruby Evelyn (45) – injured, died 12 May 1941 at BRI

Harvey, Charles Herbert – Firewatcher (65)

Hemingway, Frederick – Firewatcher (53)

Hempsall, Marion (57)

Higham, Lilian (27) – injured, died at BHC

Hill, Dorothy Peck (mother, 22)
   Hill, Barbara (daughter, 22 months)

Hopper, Elsie (30)

Horsfall, James Robert (72)

Jackson, Charles Thomas (39) – injured, died at BRI

Jackson, David (46)

Jameson, Thomas Henry – Firewatcher (59)

Kelly, Mary (56)

King, Walter Earl – Fireman, AFS (40) – injured, died at BRI

Lamb, William (46)

Land, Amelia (mother, 74)
   Kirby, Annie Elizabeth (daughter, 31)
   Kirby, Edward (son of Annie, 4)
   Kirby, Jean (daughter of Annie, 2)

Leaming, Lily (64)

Ledger, James Ashton (31) – injured, died at BRI

Leonard, Walter (61)

Lowrey, Joseph – Leading Fireman, AFS (29) – injured, died 17 May 1941 at BRI

McCabe, James (55) – injured, died 25 May 1941 at RISB:

McPherson, Veronica (9)

Marshall, George William Capes – Firewatcher (33)

Marshall, Thomas (64)

Mawson, William (42) – assumed injured, died at BHB

May, Reginald (44)

Mears, Bertie William (husband, 50)
   Mears, Gertrude (wife, 50)
   Mears, Irene Gertrude (daughter, 20)

Merrikin, Alice Gertrude (67)

Midgley, Albert (husband, 66)
   Midgley, Elizabeth (wife, 62)

Moorhouse, Nellie (sister, 21)
   Moorhouse, Fanny (sister, 18)
   Moorhouse, George (sister, 8)

Morriss, Annie Livingston – ARW (sister-in-law[35], 56)
   Morriss, Mary (sister-in-law, 62) – injured, died 10 May 1941 at BRI

Moss, Lilian (sister, 12)
   Moss, Joseph (brother, 10)
   Moss, Leonard (brother, 4)

Mountain, Johnny (grandfather, 75)
   Mountain, Sidney Albert (grandson, 16)

Needley, Roy – Constable, HCP (27)

Newell, Rachael Doris – WVS (40) – injured, died 12 May 1941 at Seacroft Hospital, Leeds

Peterson, Carl Axel – Swedish national (69) – died at RISB

Phillips, Audrey May (13)

Pike, Henry Jackson (61) – assumed injured, died 10 May 1941 at BRI

Porteous, Albert – Firewatcher (48)

Postill, Rose (mother, 24)

Pottage, Herbert (41)

Reed, Tom (father, 40)
   Reed, Marjorie (daughter, 15)

Reed, Allan (son, 4)
Reed, Betty (daughter, 2)
Rice, Annie (61)
Richardson, Leonora Catherine (daughter, 34 home)
    Richardson, Margaret Ann (daughter of Leonora, 2)
    Richardson, Sheila Mary (daughter of Leonora, 5)
Rimmington, William Watson (father, 39)
    Rimmington, Betty (daughter, 6)
Russell, Gladys (17)
Rustill, Janet Anderson (mother, 46)
    Rustill, Brenda (daughter, 11)
    Rustill, Patricia (daughter, 18 months)
Sceal, Nelson (husband, 35)
    Sceal, Elizabeth (wife, 34)
Shepherdson, Edward – ARW (43)
Smith, Gladys (40)
Smith, Hannah Lawson (53) – injured, died at BRI
Smith, William George (husband, 43)
    Smith, Annie Teresa (wife, 37)
Staples, Ada (55)
Stephenson, Walter (father, 34)
Stephenson, Terence Walter (son, 6)
Stokes, Ada (64)
Stow, Sidney (8 months)
Stubbs, Amy (mother, 32)
    Stubbs, Geoffrey (son, 19 months)
Such, James William (44)
Sutherland, Donald George – Home Guard, Firewatcher (18)
Taylor, Frances (mother, 31)
    Taylor, Douglas (son, 5)
Thompson, Amy (mother, 49)
    Thompson, Celia (daughter, 19)
    Grindall, Kenneth – Leading Seaman, HMS Westminster, Royal Navy (fiancé of Celia,[36] 21)
    Redepenning, Auguste (married to Amy's sister,[37] 67)
Thompson, Thomas William (father, 52)
    Thompson, Wilfred (son, 27)
Tomlinson, George (14)
Wade, Mary Ann Elizabeth (80)
Wadforth, Sarah Ann (64)
Wardrop, Gladys (mother, 40)
    Wardrop, Alexander (son, 15)
    Wardrop, Shirley (daughter, 5)
Webster, Harry (42)
White, Thomas Robert (58) – assumed injured, died 10 May 1941 at BRI:
Withers, John Philip (86)
Wood, Charles (36)
Woodhouse, Frederick (37)

## 10/11 May 1941

Allerston, Henry (68)
Epton, John Thomas – Firewatcher (61)
Gardner, George (64)
Hadley, John Edward (36)
Smith, Elizabeth Mary (56) – assumed injured, died at BRI
White, Albert (68)
Wormald, Frederic William (39)

## 15 to 21 May 1941

The following deaths cannot be attributed to air raid activity. Eleanor Mason and Scott may have been injured elsewhere, while William Mason and Webber may have been involved in rescue work.
Died 15 May 1941 at Little Humber Street:
    Mason, William – Firewatcher (69)
Died 16 May 1941 at 33 Little Mason Street:
    McKee, Lewis (65)
    White, Etty (65)
Died 17 May 1941 at BRI:
    Mason, Eleanor Ann (63)
18 May 1941 RISB:
    Scott, Frederick Walter (44)
Died 21 May 1941 at Orange Shed, Albert Dock:
    Webber, Ernest – Firewatcher (56)

## 2/3 June 1941

Denton, Minnie (63)
Douglas, Ethel May (husband, 17)
Douglas, Henry (wife, 28)
Elliott, George Herbert (18)
Elston, Robert William (husband, 52)
    Elston, Ellen Mary (wife, 47)
    Elston, Bertha (daughter, 25)
    Elston, Ellen (daughter, 23)
    Elston, Edna May (daughter, 18)
    Elston, Arthur (son, 17)
    Elston, Vera (daughter, 6)
Hewer, Kathleen Florence (26)
Jones, Elinor Elizabeth (78)
Martindale, Minnie (21)
Millward, Muriel (mother, 39)
Millward, Muriel Millicent (daughter, 20) – injured, died 04 June 1941 at BRI
Pearson, Beatrice Clara Ann (mother, 53)
    Pearson, Beatrice Leila (daughter, 28)
Pike, Florence Annie (32)
Richardson, John Thomas (32)
Stamford, Annie (mother, 65)
    Stamford, Irene (daughter, 33)
Stephenson, George Edgar (husband, 59)
    Stephenson, Edith Mary (wife, 59) – injured, died at BRI

Tomlinson, Walter (brother, 53)
  Tomlinson, Ernest William (brother, 46)
  Tomlinson, Hilda (sister, 42)
  Tomlinson, Amy (sister, 39)

**15 June 1941**
Firth, Thomas Henry (63) [38]

**29 June 1941**
Smith, James – Assistant Chief Constable, HCP (54) – injured, died at HRI

**1 July 1941**
Tidswell, James (50) – assumed previously injured, died at ARI

**11 July 1941**
Butterfield, William Roy – ARW (24) – assumed injured, died 26 February 1943 at 107 Welbeck Avenue
Clark, Claire Elizabeth (husband, 24)
  Clark, Herbert (wife, 27)
Cressey, Edith Annie (48)
Curtis, Fred William, M.P.S. – FAP Member (25)
Deyes, Herbert – FAP Member (44)
Dick, Francis Norman – FAP Leader, St John Ambulance Brigade (37)
Gall, Elizabeth (76) – injured, died 05 October 1941 at Pinderfields Emergency Hospital, Wakefield
Jepsen, Niels Marius – Merchant Navy, *SS Frigga* (31)
Langhorn, Harry (39) – injured, same day at BRI
Lawson, Edward – FAP Member (52)
Marshall, Ann Elizabeth (55)
Owen, Robert Gordon (2)
Pearson, Emily Amelia (70)
Peat, James William– ARP Cyclist Messenger (18)
Rispin, John – ARW (32)
Rusling, Annie Elizabeth (wife, 61)
  Rusling, Fred (husband, 60)
Strafford, Norman – ARP Ambulance Driver (31)
Taaffe, James (64)
Waller, Ernest – Ambulance Officer, Casualty Service, St John Ambulance Service (36)
Warriner, Fred (husband, 60)
  Warriner, Margaret (wife, 61)

**15 July 1941**
Airey, Ellen (49)
  Cook, Madge (a.k.a. Airey,[39] 13)
Dawson, Almena Blanche (46)
Dixon, Norah (58)

Falkingham, William Bernard (58)
Garbutt, Herbert Henry (63)
Graystone, Kate (62) – injured, died 16 July 1941 at BRI
Harrison, Richard Nelson (38)
Jacklin, Raymond (26)
Kilgar, Mary (12)
Leach, Freeman William (47) – injured, died at BHC
Lightowler, Alfred (83)
McNally, Harriet Ann (wife, 46)
  McNally, Joseph (husband, 44)
Mitchell, Beryl May (sister, 4)
  Mitchell, Hilary (sister, 2)
Moody, James Edward (68)
Pratt, Harry (husband, 72)
  Pratt, Louisa (wife, 46 – DAH
Skelton, Elizabeth (80)
Smith, George Henry (husband, 21)
  Smith, Mary Matilda (wife, 19)
Tether, Ann (65) – injured, died at BHC
Waud, Frederick (7)
Woolhouse, Harold Edgar (16)

**17/18 July 1941**
Adamson, Gertrude (daughter, 34)
  Adamson, Leonard (son of Gertrude, 15)
Allison, Isabel Gertrude (52)
Baker, Sarah Elizabeth (mother, 42)
  Baker, Marlene (daughter, 3)
Beacock, Joseph (husband, 35)
  Beacock, Betty (wife, 33)
Beckett, Alfred – Firewatcher (63) – injured, died 26 July 1941 at BHB
Bell, Gladys (mother, 20)
  Bell, Carolyn (daughter, 20 months)
Bell, Harry (husband, 51)
  Bell, Rosetta Irene (wife, 51)
  Bell, Evelyn (daughter, 21)
  Bell, Doris (daughter, 17)
  Bell, Margaret (daughter, 5 months)
Bouch, Christmas Johnson (61)
Bowen, Annie Maria (82)
Bowman, Martha Ann (grandmother, 64)
  Gilpin, Joseph (grandson, 15)
Boyes, Herbert Bilton (19)
Bradley, Harry – ARW/Firewatcher (44)
Brock, Frederick Edward (husband, 57)
  Brock, Clara (wife, 56)
Brooks, Frank (husband, 42)
  Brooks, Elsie (wife, 42)
  Brooks, Doreen (daughter, 12)
Busby, Thomas Foster (48)
Butterfield, Harold (husband, 52) – injured, died at RISB
  Butterfield, Elsie Cecilia (wife, 50)

Catterick, Bernard – Sapper, 5 Field Company, Royal Engineers (husband, 23)[40]
   Catterick, Doris (wife, 21)
Cawthorn, James Alfred (husband, 54)
   Cawthorn, Annie (wife, 52)
   Cawthorn, Audrey (daughter, 18)
Chapman, John (husband, 35)
   Chapman, Daisy (wife, 34)
   Chapman, Maureen (daughter, 2)
Cook, Kenneth (18) – assumed injured, died 19 July at HRH
Davidson, Marjorie (28)
Dilley, Emily (81)
Dixon, Hilda (42)
Donnelly, Ellen (51)
Douglas, Sarah Ann (50)
Eccles, Joseph Patrick – FAP Member (53) – injured, died at RISB
Ellis, Tom Melton (43)
Elsworth, Catherine (74)
Frost, Irene (24)
Galbraith, Archibald (husband, 51)
   Galbraith, Ruby (wife, 49)
   Galbraith, Joan (daughter, 21)
Gilroy, Michael (50) – injured, same day at HRI
Goodbarne, Frederick George Alfred (husband, 28)
   Goodbarne, Lilian (wife, 28)
   Goodbarne, Barbara (daughter, 3) – injured, same day at RISB
Harrison, Harriet (53)
Harrison, Helen (mother, 48)
   Harrison, Muriel (daughter, 17– injured, same day at HRI
Hawksley, William (husband, 67)
   Hawksley, Sarah Elizabeth (wife, 64)
   Hawksley, Walter (son, 35)
   Hawksley, Jessie[41] (wife of Walter, 40)
   Hawksley, Betty (son of Walter and Jessie, 18 months)
Heron, William (husband, 32)
   Heron, Sylvia (wife, 26)
   Heron, Valerie Rhoda (daughter, 4)
Hickson, William Edward – Firewatcher (58) – injured, died at HRH
Hilton, Robert Arthur (29)
Holland, James Henry (75) – assumed injured, died 04 May 1946 in Hull
Horncastle, Edith (mother, 58)
   Horncastle, Laura (daughter, 18)
Jackson, Margaret Ann (64) – injured, died 19 July 1941 at BHB
Jeffery, Clara (50)
Lee, Walter Henry (52)
Lewis, Thomas (53)
Lowe, Elsie May (51)

Macdonald, William (husband, 51 – DAH
   Macdonald, Florence Mary (wife, 49) – injured, died at HRI
   Macdonald, James Alfred[42] – Lance-Bombardier, 318 Battery, 30 (Surrey) Searchlight Regiment, Royal Artillery (son, 26)[43]
   Macdonald, Grace[44] (wife of James Alfred, 26)
   Macdonald, Sydney (son, 16)
   Macdonald, Jean (son, 9)
Marsh, Leonard Wright (56) – injured, died at BRI
Mason, Gertrude (44)
Matthews, John Robert (husband, 47)
   Matthews, Doris Agnes (wife, 44)
   Matthews, Colin (son, 6 months)
Melbourne, Joseph (father, 58)
   Melbourne, Kathleen (daughter, 23)
Merrylees, George (husband, 30)
   Merrylees, Violet Ida (wife, 28)
   Merrylees, Audrey (daughter, 8)
Middleton, John Thomas (husband, 62)
   Middleton, Annie (wife, 60)
   Middleton, Stella (foster-daughter, 11)
Overton, Sidney (husband, 37)
   Overton, Charlotte (wife, 37)
Peacock, Kenneth – Signalman, HMS *Ellesmere*, Royal Navy (husband, 21)[45]
   Peacock, Joan (wife, 20)
Popplestone, Maurice Alfred (19) – injured, died at RISB
Pywell, John Allan (32)
Read, Edith (48) – injured, died at HRH
Robinson, Charlotte Ellen (mother, 69)
   Robinson, William Charles (son, 46)
     Robinson, William Brumby (son of William Charles, 12)
Robinson, John Leslie – Constable, HCP (brother, 24)
   Robinson, Ronald Bertram – Police Telephone Operator (brother, 19)
Rust, Donald Albert – FAP Member (31)
Scargill, Alice Mary (husband, 55)
   Scargill, Edwin (wife, 54)
Scott, Terence (2 months)
Seaton, Jessie May (44)
Sefton, Emma (74)
South, Vincent (54)
Smith, Ada (51)
Spence, Sarah Elizabeth (31)
Spink, Catherine Helen (mother, 84)
   Spink, Ernest (son, 50) – injured, died 21 July 1941 at BHC
Stathers, Gertrude (60)
Stebbings, Catherine (37)
Stenhouse, Leonard – Firewatcher (47)

Tindall, Herbert Cyril – Firewatcher (62)
Tomlinson, John William (father, 67)
  Tomlinson, Thomas Fawcett (son, 42)
  Tomlinson, Ethel Elizabeth (wife of
  Thomas, 43)
  Tomlinson, Alan (son of Thomas and Ethel, 11)
Tran, Florence Beatrice (58)
Voss, Frederick Jacob (73)
Warrener, Alice (mother, 34
  Warrener, Kathleen (daughter, 14 months)
Waterson, Jean Rose (sister, 5)
  Waterson, Marie (sister, 3)
  Waterson, Roy (brother, 15 months)
Watts, Dorothy (36)
Webster, Dennis (8)
Whatt, Edith (46)
  Whittle, Hilary (sister, 12)
Whittle, Colon James (brother, 16 months)
Wilson, Lydia (mother, 29)
  Wilson, Ronald (son, 2)
Willoughby, William (60)
Wing, May (38)[46]
  Wing, Audrey (7)
  Wing, May (32)[47]
Wing, Peter Jason (3)
Wright, John (husband, 57)
  Wright, Effie (wife, 42)

## 23 July 1941[48]

Fletcher, Phoebe Rebecca (wife, 63)
Fletcher, Henry Barlow (husband, 62)

## 18 August 1941

Birkbeck, David Milner – ARW (father, 51)
  Birkbeck, Ada Brenda (daughter, 16)
Blackshaw, William Pitt (36)
Brown, Annie (44)
Clancy, Julia Ann (mother, 64)
  Clancy, Francis Joseph (son, Ordinary Seaman,
  HMS Pembroke, 31)[49]
  Clancy, Edna May (wife of Francis, 25)
    Clancy, Mary Ann (daughter-in-law of
    Julia[50], 22)
  Robinson, Jane (daughter of Julia, 28)
  Worsnop, Robert Joseph (grandson of Julia[51],
  18)
Cooper, Mary Isabella (59)
Dewson, Oliver Robert (husband, 74)
  Dewson, Catherine Eliza (wife, 74)
Johnson, Percy William (52)
Ryall, Norman Sidney (husband, 62)
  Ryall, Alice (wife, 62)
Southwick, Frank – Merchant Navy (37)[52]
Turner, Hilda (40)
Woodward, Reginald Horatio (63)

## 28 August 1941

Clark, Daniel – ARW (63) – injured, died 31
August 1941 at Hull

## 31 August/1 September 1941[53]

Beasty, Annie (42)
Bennett, Gertrude (mother, 44)
  Bennett, Dulcie (daughter, 17)
Camm, Doris (29)
Carron, Dorothy May (33)
Eastwood, Frances (40)
Garniss, Derek Anthony (16 months)
Harding, Ida (mother, 31)
  Harding, Ida Ann (daughter, 2)
  Harding, David Frederick (son, 5 months)
Harrison, Mavis (15)
Hotham, Reuben (67)
Hunter, Gertrude Annie – WVS (43)
Ives, Hannah (mother, 76)
  Ives, Emily (daughter, 36)
Jackson, Arthur (57)
Jarrett, Frederick – Firewatcher (30)
Johnson, Betsy Jane (79)
Kennington, Florence Ethel – WVS (45)
Leveson, Minnie – Nurse (20)
Lloyd, Francis John (73)
Lund, Gertrude Ann (mother, 56)
  Lund, Cyril (son, 18)
Lund, Thomas Edward – Home Guard
(husband, 29)
  Lund, Phyllis Nellie (wife, 28)
  Lund, Thomas James (son, 4)
  Lund, Christine Ann (daughter, 2)
Miller, Annie (66)
Oxley, Arthur (father, 27)
  Oxley, David Arthur (son, 9 months)
Parkin, Susan Cliff (67)
Roberts, Francis Percival (52)
Sanders, Ethel (aunt, 42) – injured,
died at FAP
  Sanders, Dorothy Lilian (niece, 10) – injured,
  died at HRI
Shepherd, Ernest Harrison (49)
Spence, Ada (74) – assumed injured, died
01 September 1941 at BRI
Stevens, Charlotte (50)
Thornhill, Patricia Margaret (18)
Towle, Hedley – Aircraftman 1st Class, 943
Balloon Squadron, Royal Air Force [Auxiliary
Air Force] (husband, 46)[54]
  Towle, Elsie (wife, 40)
  Towle, Hedley (son, 18)
  Towle, Betty May (daughter, 16)
  Towle, Audrey (daughter, 4)
Trotter, Maurice Alexander (9) – assumed
injured, died 01 September 1941 at BHC

Twidale, Sydney (husband, 36)
Twidale, Alice (wife, 33)

## 1 November 1941
Markham, Annie Elizabeth (60)

## 24 November 1941
March, John Henry – Section Leader, Hull Fishing Vessels Association Fire Service (54)

## 8 January 1942
Campbell, Margaret (55)

## 13/14 April 1942
Fowler, Charlotte Kate (grandmother, 61)[55]
   Fowler, Anne (granddaughter, 2)[56]
Roberts, Wilfred Bellwood (husband, 42)
   Roberts, Elva (wife, 43) – injured, died 17 April 1942 at ARI
   Roberts, Kathleen (daughter, 21) – injured, died 15 April 1942 at ARI
   Roberts, Elizabeth (daughter, 15) – injured, died at ARI
Rose, Nellie Irene (28) – assumed injured, died 17 April 1942 at ARI

## 1 May 1942
Calvert, Arthur Sainsbury (69)
Humphrey, Harold, M.M.[57] (husband, 44) – injured, died 04 May 1942 at VHSC
   Humphrey, Mary Elizabeth (wife, 42)
   Humphrey, Audrey (daughter, 14)
   Humphrey, Laurence (son, 8 – DAH[58])
Jenkinson, Anne Elizabeth (61)
Julian, Henry (brother, 68)
Julian, John Sidney (brother, 61)

## 20 May 1942
Boothby, Ada Florence (mother, 24)
   Boothby, Margaret Edith (daughter, 2)
   Boothby, Ida (sister-in-law, 22)
   Greaves, Edith ("aunt,"[59] 82)
Carr, Cecilia (17)
Clarkson, Walter William (father, 56)
   Clarkson, Walter William (son, 17)
Day, William – Firewatcher (60) – injured, died 11 August 1942 at RISB
Dearnley, Agnes Maud (mother, 56)
   Dearnley, Sydney – Home Guard (son, 17)
   Dearnley, Kathleen Pamelia (daughter, 15)
Ehlert, Mary Elizabeth (73)
Epworth, Ivy (22)
Gillis, Delphine (9 months)
Ginley, John – Firewatcher (53)
Gower, Hilda Elizabeth (41)
Hawksley, John William (65)

Hayler, Benjamin John (husband, 69)
   Hayler, Sarah Jane (wife, 51)
   Hayler, Lily Florence May (daughter, 30)
   Hayler, Violet (daughter, 22)
   Hayler, Margaret Elizabeth (daughter, 21)
   Boothby, Annie Frances (married daughter, 26)
   Holland, Ivy (married daughter, 24)
   King, George William ("uncle,"[60] 45)
Jubb, Evison (64)
Kendrew, Enid (wife, 35)
Kendrew, Sydney (husband, 35)
Levy, Abraham (54)
McAllister, Sarah (77)
McCoid, Richard Whitfield (father, 67
   McCoid, Bernard (son, 17)
McNally, James (53)
Maddison, Irene (20)
Marshall, Irene Winifred Dudgeon (mother, 39)
   Marshall, June (daughter, 11 months)
Matthews, Ada (mother, 50)
   Matthews, Robert Stephen (son, 20)
Norrie, Eileen (8)
Porter, Ernest (41)
Smith, Charles William (brother, 55)
   Smith, John (brother, 50)
Strachan, Margaret Craig (mother, 48)
   Strachan, Margaret (daughter, 19)
   Strachan, John McIntosh (son, 6)
Swift, Victor (78)
Weaver, Edith Ellen (43)

## 24 July 1942
Jubb, Harry (24) – injured, died at ARI

## 31 July/1 August 1942
Green, Frank Pattison (husband, 50)
   Green, Rose Hannah (wife, 41)
   Green, Margaret Mary (daughter, 18)
   Green, Herbert Edward (son, 14)
Inman, Harry (husband, 51)
   Inman, Eva (wife, 48)
   Inman, Edith Amelia (daughter, 17)
   Inman, Elsie May (daughter, 14)
   Inman, Leonard (son, 12)
   Stephenson, Molly (married daughter, 19)
Newland, Robert Holmes (husband, 48)
   Newland, Florence Gertrude (wife, 36)
   Newland, Florence Gertrude (daughter, 13)
   Newland, Lilian Mary (daughter, 11)
   Newland, Shirley Ann (daughter, 6)
   Newland, Robert (son, 3)
Noble, Albert Henry Charles (husband, 65)
   Noble, Sarah Ann (wife, 61)
Ryalls, John (brother, 21)
   Ryalls, Gerald Anthony (brother, 19)
   Ryalls, Dennis (brother, 16)

Ryalls, Herbert Patrick (brother, 13)
Stephenson, Stanley (30)
Turner, Joseph William (64)

## 24/25 October 1942
Briggs, Charles William – ARW (59)

## 18 November 1942
Connaughton, Thomas William – Firewatcher
(37)[61]

## 20/21 December 1942
Annison, Edward Spicer (47)
Raper, Daniel Stanley (brother, 6)
    Raper, Christine (sister, 4)

## 23/24 June 1943
Cain, David (48)
Caley, Arthur Maitland (50)
Hathaway, Joseph (74)
    Jumps, Holgate (husband, 71)
Jumps, Minnie (wife, 66)
Levesley, Doris – WVS (wife, 44)
    Levesley, Fred – Home Guard (husband , 42)
Macdonald, Maud (56)
Owens, Lillian Eliza (mother, 46)
    Owens, Mary Margaret – ARP Cyclist
    Messenger (daughter, 17)
    Owens, James Roberts (son, 15)
Prissick, Edith (mother, 36)
    Prissick, David Robin (daughter, 2)
Richardson, John William (husband, 57)
    Richardson, Mary Ann – WVS (wife, 48) –
    injured, died 25 June 1943 at RISB
Rutherford, William (62)
Shirtliff, Victor (24) – injured, died at BRI
Teece, John Campbell (44)
Tong, John (husband, 60)
    Tong, Edith (wife, 58) – injured, died 27 June
    1943 at RISB
Walkington, David (husband, 63)
    Walkington, Elizabeth (wife, 56)
    Walkington, Elsie (daughter, 22)
    Paddison, Brenda (granddaughter,[62] 10)

## 13/14 July 1943
Bilton, Mary Ellen (63) – assumed injured, died
at HRH
Cherry, Maud Annie (mother, 52) – injured, died
05 September 1943 at The Emergency Hospital,
Winwick
    Cherry, Marion (daughteR, 13)
Darley, Fred (38) – injured, died at BRI
Everington, Walter (64)

Fenton, Irene (mother, 27)
    Fenton, Jean (daughter, 3 months)
Holmes, Samuel (69) – died 24 October 1943
at BRI
Morritt, Henrietta (husband, 64)
    Morritt, George (wife, 61)
Reed, Richard (58)
Robinson, Edith Annie – WVS (49)
Robinson, Ivy Mary (mother, 33)
    Robinson, Dennis Ernest (son, 10)
    Robinson, Kenneth Ronald (son, 2)
Rodin, Rosario – Yugoslav Merchant Navy (39)
– injured, died at HRH [63]
Sandall, Garry Jackson (brother, 7)
    Sandall, David Walton (brother, 6)
Shepherd, William (34)
Shepherdson, Eva (mother, 45)
    Shepherdson, Ernest (husband, 44)
    Shepherdson, Charles (son, 16)
    Shepherdson, Edith (daughter, 14)
    Shepherdson, Margaret Rose (daughter, 8)
    Shepherdson, Muriel (daughter, 2)
Spaven, Henrietta (14)
Watson, Florence (50)
Willis, Elizabeth Ann (75)

## 11 October 1943
    Leaper, William Houldsworth – LNER
    Dockyard Fire Guard (56) – injured, died 02
    June 1944 at Sutton Annexe[64]

## 12 August 1944
McGuire, Henry – ARW (52) – injured, died 24
September 1944 at 20 Malm Street[65]

## 31 December 1944
Duncan, Albert George – Fireman, NFS (53)[66]

## 17/18 March 1945
Coggle, Walter Harold (54)
Duncan, Stanley – Second Lieutenant, Royal
Northumberland Fusiliers (21) [67]
Greenacre, William Henry – ARW (58)
Howard, Maud (34) – injured, died 21 March
1945 at RISB
McCloud, John (73)
Martin, Lily (wife, 41)
    Martin, George Ernest (husband, 33)
Ollerenshaw, James (49) – injured, died at RISB
Reed, John (71)
Steels, Ada Elizabeth (35)
Wells, Ernest (brother, 13)
    Wells, Brian (brother, 9)
Winter, Pamela Iris (21 months)

# Appendix 2
# Luftwaffe Casualties Buried in East Yorkshire

**Brandesburton (St. Mary) Churchyard**

30 April 1941
Schumacher, Josef
08 May 1941
Hoffmann, Alfred
Decker, Hermann
Kalle, Jakob
Kaminski, Johannes
London, Willi
Lorenz, Rudolf
Reinelt, Guenter
Stieglitz, Hans-Jacob
26 July 1943
Colve, Hans-Ulrich
Gabriel, Helmut
Pilger, Fritz
Trodler, Rudolf

**Hull Northern Cemetery**

14 July 1943
Pankuweit, Hugo
22 September 1943
Ehemann, Arno
Rumpff, Helmut
Stiegler, Kurt
Vom Weg, Siegfried
02 October 1943
Beubler, Guenther
Fischer, Albert
Pausch, Erwin
Urban, Heinz

# Appendix 3
# Luftwaffe Targeting Documents

| 1 | | 2 | 3 | 4 | 5 | 6 |
|---|---|---|---|---|---|---|
| **Kingston-upon-Hull** (Hull) | | 53° 45′ N 0° 20′ W | — | 162 m W | Nr. 10 | **E 07** |

Entfernung:
Spurn Head   35 km

Kingston-upon-Hull (314 000 Einw.) liegt an einer Biegung des River Humber zu beiden Seiten des von N in den Humber mündenden R i v e r  H u l l. Der Hafen besteht aus mehreren Docks, die sich zu beiden Seiten der Hull-Mündung parallel zum Humber erstrecken. Es sind von O nach W:

    a) G e o r g e  V  D o c k mit großem Getreidesilo am Westende,
    b) A l e x a n d r a  D o c k,
    c) V i c t o r i a  D o c k,
    d) 2 C i t y  D o c k s, die in einem ehemaligen Mündungsarm des River Hull nach N reichen, das auf den Karten noch verzeichnete 3. Dock im NO ist heute zugeschüttet und tritt als auffällige Parkanlage (l) hervor,
    e) A l b e r t  u n d  W. W r i g h t  D o c k,
    f) A n d r e w  D o c k.
    Außerdem treten markant hervor:
    g) die Betriebsstofflager und Raffinerie von S a l t e n d,
    h) die zahlreichen Industrieanlagen zu beiden Seiten des River Hull, unter ihnen z w e i g r o ß e  G e t r e i d e m ü h l e n (i).

Zur Orientierung innerhalb der Stadt können neben dem River Hull mit den Industriebauten drei Parkanlagen dienen:

    der W e s t p a r k (k),
    der Z e n t r a l p a r k (l),
    der O s t p a r k (m).

## E 07   Kingston-upon-Hull

Abb. 1 **Kingston-upon-Hull,** a George V Dock, b Alexandra Dock, c Victoria Dock, d City Docks, e Albert und W. Wright Dock, f Andrew Dock, g Tanklager und Raffinerie von Saltend mit zwei Brücken, h Industrieanlagen zu beiden Seiten des River Hull, i zwei große Getreidemühlen am River Hull, k Westpark, l der Zentralpark, m Ostpark

**Kingston-upon-Hull  E 07**

Abb. 2 **Kingston-upon-Hull von Osten.** g Saltend, a George V Dock, b Alexandra Dock, c Victoria Dock, e Albert und W. Wright Dock

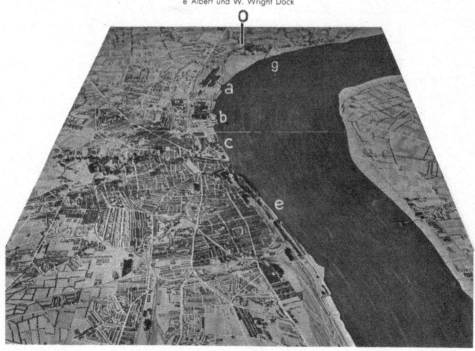

Abb. 3 **Kingston-upon-Hull von Westen.** g Saltend, a George V Dock, b Alexandra Dock, c Victoria Dock, e Albert und W. Wright Dock

## E 07  Kingston-upon-Hull

Abb. 4  Das **Tanklager von Saltend,** Raffinerie (g) und zwei Ölpiers, F l u g p l a t z im Hintergrund links (o)

Abb. 5  **George V Dock,** im Vordergrund großes Getreidesilo (si), rechts in der Mitte die Tanklager von
Saltend mit Raffinerie (g), im Hintergrund Flugplatz (o)

Abb. 6  Blick nach NW über **George V Dock** mit Getreidesilo (si), a — a die Einfahrt zum Dock

Abb. 7  Blick über das **Alexandra Dock,** mehrere Kohlenkräne (kr), links Holzstapelplätze. Markant die in den Fluß vorgebaute Brücke. Vorne rechts zwei Trockendocks

# E 07 Kingston-upon-Hull

Abb. 8 Blick nach NO über das **Alexandra Dock**. Im Vordergrund die markante, in den Fluß vorgebaute Brücke

Abb. 9 Blick über das **Victoria Dock** (Holzstapelplätze) zu den großen Mühlenwerken (i) am Hull, im Hintergrund links Zentralpark (l) (auf den Karten noch als Dock bezeichnet)

**Kingston-upon-Hull  E 07**

Abb. 10  Blick auf die **Hullmündung,** im Hintergrund große Mühlenwerke (i)

Abb. 11  Blick flußabwärts auf die **Fabriken am Hull,** im Vordergrund G a s a n s t a l t

# E 07 Kingston-upon-Hull

Abb. 12 Blick auf die **Fabriken am Hull** am N-Rand der Stadt. Im Hintergrund die Gasanstalt (s. Abb. 11)

Abb. 13 Blick nach NNW auf die beiden **City Docks** (d) und die **Mündung des Hull** (hu), der Zentralpark (l) (auf den Karten noch als Dock verzeichnet), G ü t e r b a h n h o f (bf$_1$), dahinter das Eisenbahndock, durch die hohen Lagerhäuser hinter dem Bahnhof verdeckt, Hauptbahnhof (bf$_2$)

Abb. 14  Blick nach NO auf das Ostende des **Albert Dock,** Einfahrt zu den City Docks (d), Güter-
bahnhof (bf₁), links davon die hohen Lagerhäuser am Eisenbahndock

Abb. 15  Blick über das **Andrew Dock** vorne und das Albert Dock (hinten)

## E 07  Kingston-upon-Hull

Abb. 16  Blick über das **Andrew Dock,** links ein großer Verschiebebahnhof

Abb. 17  Blick über den **Westpark**

Abb. 18  Blick über den **Ostpark**

# Bibliography

## Publications

Dobinson, Colin, *Fields of Deception* (York: Methuen, 2013).

Geraghty, T., *A North-East Coast Town* (Hull: Hull Corporation, 1951).

Haldane, J.B.S., *A.R.P.* (London: Victor Gollancz, 1938).

Langdon-Davies, John, *Air Raid: The Technique of Silent Approach* (London: Routledge, 1938).

Ludlam, A.J., *Railways to New Holland and the Humber Ferries* (Headington: The Oakwood Press, 1996).

Ogley, Bob, *Doodlebugs and Rockets: The Battle of the Flying Bombs* (Kent, Froglets Publications, 1992).

Mee, Arthur (ed.), *The King's England: East Yorkshire with York* (London: Hodder and Stoughton, 1941).

Norman, Bill, *Broken Eagles: Luftwaffe Losses over Yorkshire 1939–1945* (Barnsley: Pen & Sword Ltd, 2001).

Tennant, Alan J., *British and Commonwealth Merchant Ship Losses to Axis Submarines 1939–1945* (Stroud: Sutton Publishing Ltd, 2001).

## The National Archives, Kew

AIR 2/2878: CAMOUFLAGE (Code B, 18): Dummy aerodromes

AIR 27/2287: 942 Balloon Squadron, Royal Air Force, Summary of Events

AIR 27/2288: 942/943 Balloon Squadron, Royal Air Force, Summary of Events

AN 2/1103 – 1117: Railway Executive Committee, Daily Reports Parts 9–23

HO 186/1861: Hull air raids, reports on nightly trekkers scheme.

HO 192/131: Air Raid Damage, Region No. 2, Hull, 30 April – 1 May 1942

HO 192/156: Air Raid Damage, Region No. 2, Hull, 23–24 June 1943

HO 198/138: Bomb Census Papers, Various Reports, 23–24 June 1943 to 20/21 Mar 1945

HO 198/160: Bomb Census Papers, monthly fall of bombs recorded by Bomb Census prior to September 1941

HO 199/45: Hull and East Riding Information Committee, observations on working of post-raid organisations following air attack 18 July 1941.

HO 199/326: Hull, consolidated report on the effects of heavy air attacks on 7/8 and 8/9 May 1941.

HO 199/453: Enemy bombing, investigation of its effects on production, transport and morale

HO 201/1 – 16: Key Points Intelligence Directorate, Daily Reports, Volumes 1–16

HO 250/21 – 86: Home Office: Inter-departmental Committee on Civil Defence Gallantry Awards, Copies of evidence, batches 21 to 86

WO 166/2464: 173 Heavy Anti-Aircraft Battery (HAA)

WO 166/2546: 266 Heavy Anti-Aircraft Battery (HAA)

WO 166/2565: 286 Heavy Anti-Aircraft Battery (HAA)

# Notes

## A City Apart

1 The south-east extension was not added until after the Second World War.
2 Ludlam, 1996, p. 29.
3 'Strengthening New Holland Railway Pier', *The Engineer*, 27 October 1922, p. 450.
4 Mee, 1941, p. 163.
5 'Survivors at the Foreign Office.' *The Times*, 25 October 1904, p. 7, columns 6–7.
6 This included this writer's grandfather, Stabley Rothwell, before he returned to Merchant Navy service in 1942.
7 www.hullcc.gov.uk/museumcollections/collections/storydetail.php?irn=692&master=442
8 Mee, 1941, pp. 173–4.

## Prelude

1 Renamed Hull Minster in May 2017.
2 'Mr Baldwin on Aerial Warfare.' *The Times*: 11 November 1932, p. 7.
3 'History Making British Film for Hull Next Week.' *Hull Daily Mail*, 4 July 1936, p. 7, column 1.
4 A French version was also produced.
5 www.iwm.org.uk/collections/item/object/1122
6 Langdon-Davies, 1938.
7 Haldane, 1938, pp. 20–3.
8 Haldane, 1938, p. 68.
9 Haldane, 1938, p. 191.
10 See Appendix 4.
11 http://map.princeton.edu/mapviewer/#/br86b5285
12 '300,000 gas-Masks in Hull by to-morrow.' *Hull Daily Mail*, 22 September 1938, p. 7, column 3.

13 'Hull's 46 more ARP workers.' *Hull Daily Mail*, 23 September 1938, p. 7, column 5.
14 'Hull needs more Specials.' *Hull Daily Mail*, 23 September 1938, p. 9, column 4.
15 'Hull must have 4,000 ARP workers.' *Hull Daily Mail*, 24 September 1938, p. 9, column 4.
16 'Organising Hull for ARP.' *Hull Daily Mail*, 24 September 1938, p. 5, columns 1–2.
17 'Hull ARP Committee asks for vacant land to build shelters.' *Hull Daily Mail*, 26 September 1938, p. 1, column 6.
18 'Bomb-proof shelters planned to protect every citizen in Hull.' *Hull Daily Mail*, 26 September 1938, p. 4, columns 3–4.
19 Ibid.
20 Ibid.
21 'Hull's House-to-House Gas-Mask Delivery to Begin To-morrow.' *Hull Daily Mail*, 27 September 1938, p. 7, columns 2–3.
22 'Hull's Air Raid Buzzer.' *Hull Daily Mail*, 29 September 1938, p. 1, column 6.
23 www.hullfair.net/ui/historyhome.htm
24 'Hull Civic Heads at Opening of City's Annual Carnival.' *Hull Daily Mail*, 11 October 1938, p. 1, columns 1–3.
25 'Welcome to the Fair.' *Hull Daily Mail*, 11 October 1938, p. 8, column 3.
26 www.17balloons.co.uk/pages/page-04.html
27 AIR 2/2878.
28 WO 166/2464.
29 WO 166/2546.
30 WO 166/2565.
31 'Exodus of Hull's 50,000 Children Goes On With Clockwork Precision.' *Hull Daily Mail*, 1 September 1939, p. 4, columns 4–6.
32 www.cwgc.org/find-war-dead/casualty/2497554/

33 'Five Hull Men Went Down in *Courageous*.' *Hull Daily Mail*, 22 September 1939, p. 1, column 7.

34 www.cwgc.org/find-war-dead/casualty/2475696/

35 www.cwgc.org/find-war-dead/casualty/2369517/

36 www.cwgc.org/find-war-dead/casualty/2477966/

37 www.cwgc.org/find-war-dead/casualty/2479718/

38 www.cwgc.org/find-war-dead/casualty/2489574/

39 'Hull Fair Cancelled.' *Hull Daily Mail*, 30 September 1939, p. 3, column 3.

40 'Biggest Hull Fair Opens Tomorrow.' *Hull Daily Mail*, 10 October 1945, p. 1, columns 5–6.

41 'Hull People and the Dutch Are Closely Tied by Bonds of Friendship.' *Hull Daily Mail*, 11 October 1940, p. 4, columns 2–4.

42 'Rifle Fired by Accident.' *Hull Daily Mail*, 1 June 1940, p. 4, column 5.

43 www.cwgc.org/find-war-dead/casualty/2402318/

44 'Four Hull Trawlers Lost in Dunkirk Withdrawal.' *Hull Daily Mail*, 4 June 1940, p. 1, columns 1–2.

## Overture: June 1940 To February 1941

1 HO 201/1: *Damage Appreciation 19-20/06/40*, pp. 2–3.

2 Ibid.

3 AIR 27/2287: 19 June 1940 entry and June 1940, Appendix E.

4 *Supplement to the London Gazette*, 30 September 1940, p. 5768.

5 'Germans Claim Hull Oil Tanks Set on Fire.' *Hull Daily Mail*, 20 June 1940, p. 1, column 5.

6 'Yorkshire Defence Put Up a Great Show.' *Hull Daily Mail*, 20 June 1940, p. 1, columns 3–4.

7 Norman, 2001, pp. 37–8.

8 Geraghty, 1951, p. 109.

9 AIR 27/2287: 25 June entry.

10 Norman, 2001, pp. 40–2.

11 AIR 27/2287: 11 July entry.

12 Geraghty, 1951, p. 109.

13 Ibid.

14 HO 201/1: *Damage Appreciation 24-25/08/40*, p. 7.

15 Geraghty, 1951, p. 109.

16 HO 201/1: *Damage Appreciation 26-27/08/40*, p. 5.

17 HO 201/1: *Damage Appreciation 28-29/08/40*, p. 6.

18 Geraghty, 1951, p. 109. This erroneously refers to 'Seward Goods Station'.

19 This ran parallel to and to the east of the south end of Williamson Street, subsequently obliterated by redevelopment or clearance, and not on the site of the nearby Bellamy Court.

20 Geraghty, 1951, p. 109.

21 Both are buried at the German Military Cemetery at Cannock Chase, Staffordshire.

22 Norman, 2001, pp. 62–4.

23 HO 201/2: *Damage Appreciation 02-03/09/40*, p. 4. This states the time at 00:09, which seems to be a confusion with the start of the appropriate Red Warning period.

24 Geraghty, 1951, p. 109.

25 Ibid.

26 Ibid.

27 'Mother of Four Killed by Bomb in North-East Town.' *Hull Daily Mail*, 14 October 1940, p. 1, columns 6–7.

28 AIR 27/2287: 22 October entry.

29 Geraghty, 1951, p. 109. This gives the locations as 'Sutton and Silverdale Road, Maybury Road, Bellfield Avenue,' but there were no known PMs before May 1941 in the vicinity of the last two, although there were several either side of Sutton Road on the east side of the River Hull.

30 HO 201/3: *Damage Appreciation 21-22/10/40*, p. 8.

31 HO 201/4: *Damage Appreciation 08-09/11/40*, p. 4.

32 Geraghty, 1951, p. 109.

33 Geraghty, 1951, p. 110.

34 Ibid.

35 'Amy Johnson's Car Light Fine.' *Hull Daily Mail*, 4 October 1939, p. 3, column 5.

36 http://afleetingpeace.org/the-ata/index.php/9-lists

37 'Speedboats' Vain Search for Amy Johnson.' *Hull Daily Mail*, 7 January 1941, p. 1, columns 5–6.

38 Geraghty, 1951, p. 110.

39 Ibid.

40 Ibid.

41 Ibid.

42 Ibid.

43 HO 250/21/894.

44 *Supplement to the London Gazette*, 25 April 1941, p. 2337.
45 Geraghty, 1951, p. 110.
46 Geraghty, 1951, p. 110.

## Crescendo: March To July 1941

1 Ibid.
2 Ibid.
3 Norman, 2001, p. 81.
4 HO 250/24/1022.
5 *Supplement to the London Gazette*, 27 June 1941, p. 3648.
6 'Hull Fire-Watcher Wins British Empire Medal.' *Hull Daily Mail*, 28 June 1941, p. 1, columns '5–6.
7 Geraghty, 1951, p. 110.
8 Geraghty, 1951, p. 110.
9 HO 250/27/1094.
10 Geraghty, 1951, p. 110.
11 Ibid.
12 Geraghty, 1951, p. 13.
13 *Supplement to the London Gazette*, 2 September 1941, p. 5139. The citation states that four people were killed at the Control Centre, but only Diamond and Garton can be placed at the location.
14 Geraghty, 1951, p. 28.
15 Geraghty, 1951, p. 110.
16 Ibid.
17 Ibid.
18 Geraghty, 1951, p. 111.
19 Immediately west of Studley Street, opposite the East Hull Public Baths.
20 *Hull at War*. South Cave: Agency Video, 1992.
21 Geraghty, 1951, p. 111.
22 Ibid.
23 Ibid.
24 Ibid.
25 Geraghty, 1951, p. 111: 98 x HE, 26≈x PM, 2 x GM.
26 HO 198/160: 107 x HE, 22 x PM, 1 x GM.
27 www.warbirdsresourcegroup.org/LRG/flamc250.htm
28 www.warbirdsresourcegroup.org/LRG/flamc500.htm
29 Island Pier – also known as Island Wharf – was the west side of the Humber Dock Basin, isolated by the Albert Channel (i.e. 'Island Creek') connecting the Basin to Albert Dock Basin.
30 www.cwgc.org/find-war-dead/casualty/2451641/
31 AIR 27/2287: 9 May 1940 entry.

32 Norman, 2001, p. 89.
33 *Supplement to the London Gazette*, 10 October 1941, p. 5839.
34 'Hull Men Fight Air Raid Fires.' *Hull Daily Mail*, 11 October 1941, p. 1, columns 5–6.
35 HO 250/35/1375A & 1375B.
36 Ibid.
37 Ibid.
38 *Supplement to the London Gazette*, 25 July 1941, p. 4256.
39 A type of small fire boat.
40 HO 250/43/1674A, 1674B & 1674C.
41 What remains of Naylor's Row today is only the northern section; the southern part met the west side of Thomas Street just north of Warwick Street.
42 HO 250/35/1374.
43 HO 250/38/1543A, 1543B, 1543C & 1543D.
44 *Supplement to the London Gazette*, 15 August 1941, p. 4706.
45 *Supplement to the London Gazette*, 15 August 1941, p. 4783.
46 HO 250/39/1529.
47 *Supplement to the London Gazette*, 22 August 1941, p. 4851.
48 *Supplement to the London Gazette*, 5 December 1941, p. 6935.
49 'Horses Saved From Blazing Stables.' *Hull Daily Mail*, 6 December 1941, p. 1, column 4.
50 HO 250/40.
51 Ibid.
52 *Supplement to the London Gazette*, 14 November 1941, p. 6557.
53 *Supplement to the London Gazette*, 26 September 1941, p. 5584.
54 HO 250/43/1670.
55 *Supplement to the London Gazette*, 26 September 1941, p. 5584.
56 On the south side of the section of Anlaby Road on the east of what is now Ferensway.
57 HO 198/160.
58 Geraghty, 1951, p. 111.
59 Dobinson, 2013, pp. 111–12.
60 Norman, 2001, pp. 89–92. Although initially buried in the churchyard at Long Riston, the two dead were subsequently moved to the German military cemetery at Cannock Chase in Staffordshire.
61 Norman, 2001, p. 95.
62 Norman 2001, pp. 92–4.
63 HO 250/39/1518A, 1518B, 1518C, 1518D & 1518E.

64  *Supplement to the London Gazette,*
    29 August 1941, p. 5002.
65  *Supplement to the London Gazette,*
    29 August 1941, p. 5003.
64  Official documentation – including the
    *London Gazette* notice – spells the surname
    as 'Colletta' in error.
67  HO 250/43/1671.
68  Ibid.
69  *Supplement to the London Gazette,*
    19 September 1941, p. 5398.
70  www.colettagardencentre.co.uk/about-us/
71  HO 250/47/1784.
72  *Supplement to the London Gazette,*
    17 October 1941, p. 6026.
73  Geraghty, 1951, pp. 52–4.
74  HO 250/43/1672A, 1672B & 1672C.
75  Ibid.
76  *Supplement to the London Gazette,*
    19 September 1941, p. 5400.
77  HO 250/35/1373A & 1373B.
78  *Supplement to the London Gazette,* 1 August
    1941, p. 4421.
79  HO 250/37/1492A & 1492B.
80  *Supplement to the London Gazette,* 8 August
    1941, pp. 4548–9.
81  HO 250/38/1493A & 1493B.
82  HO 250/39/1536.
83  *Supplement to the London Gazette,*
    26 September 1941, p. 5585.
84  Site of the modern Morrill Street Health
    Centre.
85  HO 250/51/179.
86  'More Medals for Hull Heroes.' *Hull Daily
    Mail,* 22 November 1941, p. 1, column 3.
87  Ibid.
88  HO 250/39/1517.
89  Ibid.
90  HO 250/39/1528.
91  *Supplement to the London Gazette,*
    29 August 1941, p. 5002.
92  HO 250/38/1500.
93  *Supplement to the London Gazette,*
    14 October1941, p. 6026.
94  *Supplement to the London Gazette,* 7 July
    1941, pp. 3893–4.
95  Geraghty, 1951, p. 111.
96  Ibid.
97  HO 250/52/1814
98  Geraghty, 1951, p. 111.
99  Four from the Hull City Police, and two
    from the LNER Police.
100 At the time located to the south of the
    modern School.
101 Norman, 2001, pp. 105–6.

102 Geraghty, 1951, p. 111.
103 Ibid.
104 HO 250/52/1815.
105 *Supplement to the London Gazette,*
    21 November 1941, p. 6692.
106 HO 250/51/1799.
107 *Supplement to the London Gazette,*
    21 November 1941, p. 6691.
108 HO 250/45/1767A, 1767B, 1767C.
109 *Supplement to the London Gazette,*
    10 October 1941, p. 5839.
110 'Hull Men Fight Air Raid Fires.' *Hull Daily
    Mail,* 11 October 1941, p. 1, columns 5–6.
111 HO 250/56/1845A & 1845B.
112 HO 250/52/1814.
113 HO 250/52/1845A & 1845B.
114 It is unclear which of the rescue teams found
    him, but it was probably McHugh's.
115 HO 250/52/1814.
116 HO 250/52/1845A & 1845B.
117 *Supplement to the London Gazette,*
    24 February 1942, p. 953.
118 *Supplement to the London Gazette,*
    18 November 1941, p. 6692. The citation for
    Jacklin refers to the George Street incident
    only, although the Blenheim Street one was
    also detailed in the award recommendation
    documents.
119 Dobinson, 2013, p. 133.
120 HO 199/326.
121 HO 199/45 – Appendix 3.
122 Geraghty, 1951, p. 111.
123 HO 201/10: *Damage Appreciation
    23-24/07/41,* p. 1.
124 Dobinson, 2013, p. 133.
125 HO 186/1861.
126 Ibid.
127 Ibid.
128 www.hulldailymail.co.uk/uncovered-
    amazing-schoolgirls-essays-hull-blitz/
    story-25989622-detail/story.html
129 HO 199/453.
130 Ibid.
131 Ibid.
132 HO 199/453.
133 HO 199/453.

### Finale: August 1941 To March 1945

1  'Their Majesties Inspect Hull Bomb Damage.'
   *Hull Daily Mail,* 6 August 1941, p. 1,
   column 1.
2  AIR 27/2287: 8 August entry.
3  Norman, 2001, p. 131.
4  Norman, 2001, pp. 108–10.
5  Geraghty, 1951, p. 112.

6  HO 250/48/1796.

7  *Supplement to the London Gazette*, 24 October 1941, p. 6176.

8  HO 201/11: *Weekly Report 27/08-03/09/1941*, p. 1.

9  Dobinson, 2013, p. 133.

10  Geraghty, 1951, p. 112.

11  Ibid.

12  AIR 27/2287: 4 December 1941 entry.

13  www.17balloons.co.uk/pages/page-08.html

14  *Hull at War.* South Cave: Agency Video, 1992.

15  'An Angry Seaman.' *Hull Daily Mail*, 23 February 1942, p. 3, column 6.

16  Tennant, 2001, p. 75.

17  http://uboat.net/allies/merchants/2211.html

18  Norman, 2001, p. 131.

19  AIR 27/2288: 8 March 1942 entry.

20  AIR 27/2288: March 1942 Appendix A.

21  Geraghty, 1951, p. 112.

22  HO 192/131.

23  HO 250/79/2041.

24  *Supplement to the London Gazette*, 28 July 1942, p. 3363.

25  Norman, 2001, p. 140.

26  Geraghty, 1951, p. 112.

27  HO 201/12: *Weekly Report 19-20/05/42*, p. 2.

28  The entrance to Ripon Street was approximately where the junction of Hedon Road and Mount Pleasant is.

29  HO 250/70/1932.

30  Ibid.

31  *Supplement to the London Gazette*, 15 January 1943, p. 339.

32  HO 250/72/1962.

33  *Supplement to the London Gazette*, 22 September 1942, p. 4171.

34  HO 250/72/1960.

35  *Supplement to the London Gazette*, 22 September 1942, p. 4171.

36  HO 250/78/2024.

37  Ibid.

38  *Supplement to the London Gazette*, 1 December 1942, p. 5293.

39  Geraghty, 1951, p. 112.

40  'Death after ARP Exercise,' *Hull Daily Mail*, 19/11/1942, p. 1, column 7.

41  'Death at ARP Exercise,' *Hull Daily Mail*, 21/11/1942, p. 4, column 3.

42  Geraghty, 1951, p. 112.

43  Geraghty, 1951, p. 112.

44  Norman, 2001, p. 168.

45  AIR 27/2288: 26 April 1943 entry.

46  HO 198/138.

47  Geraghty, 1951, p. 112.

48  HO 250/86/2101.

49  HO 250/78/2023.

50  *Supplement to the London Gazette*, 2 November 1943, p. 4849.

51  HO 198/138.

52  Ibid.

53  www.warbirdsresourcegroup.org/LRG/sd2.htm

54  Many live examples kept as 'souvenirs' unexpectedly turned up in the 1970s when the ITV drama series *Danger UXB* included an episode about them.

55  HO 192/156.

56  HO 198/138.

57  Norman, 2001, p. 172.

58  Geraghty, 1951, p. 112.

59  Norman, 2001, p. 183.

60  Norman, 2001, p. 184.

61  http://fliphtml5.com/lbsh/shsz/basic

62  HO 250/86/2109.

63  Ibid.

64  *Supplement to the London Gazette*, 2 November 1943, p. 4850.

65  Norman, 2001, pp. 188–90.

66  One body was recovered and buried in Grimsby (Scartho Road) Cemetery.

67  Norman, 2001, pp. 191–2.

68  Norman, 2001, pp. 193–4.

69  AIR 27/2288: 22 September 1943 entry.

70  Norman, 2001, p. 196. Norman states that only two of the crew (Uffzs Heinz Urban and Albert Fischer) were buried in Hull, when in fact all four were.

71  'Hull Fitter's Death,' *Hull Daily Mail*, 8/06/1944, p. 3, column 7.

72  'Aerial Trapeze Accident,' *Hull Daily Mail*, 30/09/1944, p. 3, column 7.

73  HO 198/138.

74  Ogley, Bob. *Doodlebugs and Rockets: The Battle of the Flying Bombs.* Westerham, Kent: Froglets Publications, 1992, pp. 168–9.

75  Geraghty, 1951, pp. 22, 72.

76  'Air Raid on N.E. Town.' *Hull Daily Mail*, 2 March 1945, p. 2, columns 5–6.

77  HO 198/138.

78  Geraghty, 1951, p. 12 states that the total number of bombs were 35 SD 10s and 35 SD 19s. In fact the former were usually transported and dropped in the AB-250-2 sub-munition container, which held 17. 'SD 19' is not a recognised Luftwaffe designation, so it seems probable that in fact the load was four containers of SD 10s, giving a total of sixty-eight bombs.

79 'Air Raid on N.E. Town.' *Hull Daily Mail*, 19 March 1945, p. 1, columns 5–6.

## Railway, Industrial And Infrastructure Damage

1 Geraghty, 1951, p. 109. This erroneously refers to the structure as 'Chapman Street Railway Bridge.'

2 Railway Executive Committee (REC): File: *D2, 18:00 19/06/40 to 06:00 20/06/40*, sheet 1 AN 2/1103]. This erroneously refers to the structure as 'Fordyke [*sic*] Stream Bridge.'

3 AN 2/1103: *D1, 06:00-18:00 20/06/40*, p. 1.

4 AN 2/1103: *D2, 18:00 19/06/40 to 06:00 20/06/40*, sheet 1.

5 AN 2/1103: *D1, 06:00-18:00 20/06/40*, p. 1.

6 AN 2/1103: *D2, 18:00 19/06/40 to 06:00 20/06/40*, sheet 2.

7 AN 2/1103: *D1, 06:00-18:00 20/06/40*, p. 1.

8 AN 2/1103: *D2, 18:00 25/06/40 to 06:00 26/06/40*, sheet 1.

9 AN 2/1103: *D2, 18:00 25/06/40 to 06:00 26/06/40*, sheet 2.

10 HO 201/1: *Damage Appreciation 01-02/07/40*, p. 1.

11 HO 201/1: *Damage Appreciation 16-17/08/40*, p. 8

12 AN 2/1103: *D2, 18:00 15/08/40 to 06:00 16/08/40*, sheet 2.

13 HO 201/1: *Damage Appreciation 16-17/08/40*, p. 5.

14 HO 201/1: *Damage Appreciation 20-21/08/40*, p. 6.

15 Geraghty, 1951, p. 109.

16 HO 201/1: *Damage Appreciation 26-27/08/40*, p. 5.

17 HO 201/1: *Damage Appreciation 28-29/08/40*, p. 6.

18 Geraghty, 1951, p. 109. This erroneously refers to 'Seward Goods Station.'

19 HO 201/1: *Damage Appreciation 29-30/08/40*, p. 10.

20 HO 201/2: *Damage Appreciation 18-19/09/40*, p. 7.

21 HO 201/3: *Damage Appreciation 13-14/10/40*, p. 4.

22 Geraghty, 1951, p. 109.

23 HO 201/4: *Damage Appreciation 01-02/11/40*, p. 8.

24 HO 201/4: *Damage Appreciation 03-04/11/40*, p. 3.

25 HO 201/4: *Damage Appreciation 01-02/11/40*, p. 5.

26 AN 2/1106: *RWD2, 18:00 10/11/40 to 06:00 11/11/40*, sheet 1.

27 HO 201/5: *Damage Appreciation 12-13/12/40*, p. 2.

28 HO 201/5: *Damage Appreciation 12-13/12/40*, p. 3.

29 AN 2/1107: *D2, 18:00 04/02/41 to 06:00 05/02/41*, sheet 1. This report erroneously refers to 'Eller Street.'

30 AN 2/1107: *D1, 06:00 to 18:00 05/02/41*, sheet 1.

31 HO 201/7: *Damage Appreciation 14-15/02/41*, p. 2.

32 HO 201/7: *Damage Appreciation 19-20/02/41*, p. 2.

33 HO 201/7: *Damage Appreciation 15-16/02/41*, p. 3.

34 AN 2/1107: *D2, 18:00 15/02/41 to 06:00 16/02/41*, sheet 1.

35 HO 201/7: *Damage Appreciation 22-23/02/41*, pp. 2–3.

36 AN 2/1107: *D2, 18:00 22/02/41 to 06:00 23/02/41*, sheet 1.

37 AN 2/1107: *D1, 06:00 to 18:00 28/02/41*, sheet 1.

38 AN 2/1107: *RWD2, 18:00 22/02/41 to 06:00 23/02/41*, sheet 1.

39 HO 201/7: *Damage Appreciation 25-26/02/41*, p. 2.

40 HO 201/7: *Damage Appreciation 04-05/03/41*, p. 2.

41 HO 201/7: *Damage Appreciation 14-15/03/41*, p. 6.

42 HO 201/7: *Damage Appreciation 16-17/03/41*, p. 6.

43 AN 2/1108: *RWD2, 18:00 13/03/41 to 06:00 14/03/41*, sheet 2.

44 AN 2/1108: *RWD1, 06:00 to 18:00 14/03/41*, sheet 2.

45 AN 2/1108: *RWD2, 18:00 13/03/41 to 06:00 14/03/41*, sheet 2.

46 AN 2/1108: *RWD1, 06:00 to 18:00 14/03/41*, sheet 2.

47 AN 2/1108: *RWD2, 18:00 13/03/41 to 06:00 14/03/41*, sheet 2.

48 HO 201/7: *Damage Appreciation 31/03-01/04/41*, p. 2.

49 AN 2/1108: *RWD2, 18:00 13/03/41 to 06:00 14/03/41*, sheet 2.

50 HO 201/7: *Damage Appreciation 14-15/03/41*, p. 5.

51 AN 2/1108: *RWD1, 06:00 to 18:00 14/03/41*, sheet 2.

52  AN 2/1108: *RWD2, 18:00 13/03/41 to 06:00 14/03/41*, sheet 1.

53  HO 201/7: *Damage Appreciation 19-20/03/41*, p. 6.

54  HO 201/7: *Damage Appreciation 19-20/03/41*, p. 7.

55  HO 201/7: *Damage Appreciation 17-18/03/41*, p. 5.

56  HO 201/7: *Damage Appreciation 19-20/03/41*, p. 16.

57  HO 201/7: *Damage Appreciation 19-20/03/41*, p. 13.

58  HO 201/7: *Damage Appreciation 20-21/03/41*, p. 9.

59  HO 201/7: *Damage Appreciation 18-19/03/41*, p. 2.

60  HO 201/7: *Damage Appreciation 18-19/03/41*, p. 1.

61  HO 201/7: *Damage Appreciation 20-21/03/41*, p. 2.

62  HO 201/7: *Damage Appreciation 24-25/03/41*, p. 3.

63  HO 201/7: *Damage Appreciation 19-20/03/41*, p. 6.

64  HO 201/7: *Damage Appreciation 20-21/03/41*, p. 9 7.

65  HO 201/7: *Damage Appreciation 24-25/03/41*, p. 5.

66  HO 201/7: *Damage Appreciation 20-21/03/41*, p. 2.

67  HO 201/7: *Damage Appreciation 20-21/03/41*, p. 2.

68  HO 201/7: *Damage Appreciation 28-29/03/41*, p. 1.

69  HO 201/8: *Damage Appreciation 03-04/04/41*, p. 2.

70  HO 201/7: *Damage Appreciation 18-19/03/41*, p. 8.

71  AN 2/1108: *D2, 18:00 18/03/41 to 06:00 19/03/41*, sheet 1.

72  AN 2/1108: *RWD1, 06:00to 18:00 21/03/41*, sheet 2.

73  AN 2/1108: *D1, 06:00to 18:00 10/04/41*, sheet 2.

74  HO 201/7: *Damage Appreciation 19-20/03/41*, p. 12.

75  AN 2/1108: *D2, 18:00 18/03/41 to 06:00 19/03/41*, sheet 1.

76  AN 2/1108: *D2, 18:00 18/03/41 to 06:00 19/03/41*, sheet 1.

77  AN 2/1108: *RWD2, 18:00 20/03/41 to 06:00 21/03/41*, sheet 1.

78  AN 2/1108: *RWD1, 06:00to 18:00 21/03/41*, sheet 2.

79  HO 201/7: *Damage Appreciation 19-20/03/41*, p. 6.

80  HO 201/8: *Damage Appreciation 08-09/04/41*, p. 4.

81  HO 201/8: *Damage Appreciation 31/03-01/04/41*, p. 1.

82  AN 2/1108: *RWD1, 06:00to 18:00 01/04/41*, sheet 1.

83  HO 201/8: *Damage Appreciation 01-02/04/41*, p. 2.

84  HO 201/8: *Damage Appreciation 31/03-01/04/41*, p. 2.

85  HO 201/8: *Damage Appreciation 07-08/04/41*, p. 5.

86  HO 201/8: *Damage Appreciation 10-11/04/41*, p. 13.

87  HO 201/8: *Damage Appreciation 11-12/04/41*, p. 7.

88  HO 201/8: *Damage Appreciation 26-27/04/41*, p. 2.

89  HO 201/8: *Damage Appreciation 15-16/04/41*, p. 3.

90  AN 2/1108: *D2, 18:00150/4/041 to 06:00 16/04/41*, sheet 2.

91  AN 2/1108: *RWD2, 18:0015/04/041 to 06:00 16/04/41*, sheet 1.

92  AN 2/1108: *D1, 06:00to 18:00 17/03/41*, sheet 1.

93  HO 201/8: *Damage Appreciation 18-19/04/41*, p. 5.

94  HO 201/8: *Damage Appreciation 24-25/04/41*, p. 4.

95  HO 201/9: *Damage Appreciation 03-04/05/41*, p. 1.

96  HO 201/9: *Damage Appreciation 05-06/05/41*, p. 5.

97  HO 201/9: *Damage Appreciation 05-06/05/41*, p. 1.

98  HO 201/9: *Damage Appreciation 05-06/05/41*, p. 6.

99  HO 201/9: *Damage Appreciation 07-08/05/41*, p. 2.

100  HO 201/9: *Damage Appreciation 08-09/05/41*, p. 2.

101  HO 201/9: *Damage Appreciation 07-08/05/41*, p. 2, 9.

102  HO 201/9: *Damage Appreciation 08-09/05/41*, p. 2.

103  HO 201/9: *Damage Appreciation 09-10/05/41*, p. 3.

104  HO 201/9: *Damage Appreciation 10-11/05/41*, p. 4.

105  HO 201/9: *Damage Appreciation 19-20/05/41*, p. 6.

106  HO 201/9: *Damage Appreciation 09-10/05/41*, p. 7.

107  HO 201/9: *Damage Appreciation 07-08/05/41*, p. 8.

108  HO 201/9: *Damage Appreciation 08-09/05/41*, p. 10.

109  HO 201/9: *Damage Appreciation 08-09/05/41*, p. 8.

110  HO 201/9: *Damage Appreciation 10-11/05/41*, p. 4.

111  HO 201/9: *Weekly Summary 11-18/06/41*, p. 2.

112  HO 201/9: *Damage Appreciation 10-11/05/41*, p. 4.

113  HO 201/9: *Damage Appreciation 10-11/05/41*, p. 8.

114  HO 201/9: *Damage Appreciation 24-25/05/41*, p. 2.

115  AN 2/1109: *D2, 18:00 11/53/41 to 06:00 12/05/41*, sheet 1.

116  HO 201/9: *Damage Appreciation 11-12/05/41*, p. 2.

117  HO 201/9: *Damage Appreciation 15-16/05/41*, p. 4.

118  HO 201/9: *Damage Appreciation 28-29/05/41*, pp. 1 & 2.

119  HO 201/9: *Damage Appreciation 28-29/06/41*, p. 1.

120  HO 201/9: *Damage Appreciation 10-11/07/41*, p. 1.

121  HO 201/9: *Damage Appreciation 10-11/07/41*, p. 2.

122  HO 201/9: *Damage Appreciation 11-12/07/41*, p. 2

123  HO 201/9: *Damage Appreciation 11-12/07/41*, p. 1.

124  HO 201/9: *Damage Appreciation 14-15/07/41*, p. 2.

125  HO 201/9: *Damage Appreciation 17-18/07/41*, p. 1.

126  HO 201/9: *Damage Appreciation 17-18/07/41*, p. 2.

127  HO 201/9: *Damage Appreciation 19-20/07/41*, p. 2.

128  HO 201/9: *Damage Appreciation 17-18/07/41*, p. 1.

129  HO 201/9: *Damage Appreciation 18-19/07/41*, p. 1.

130  HO 201/9: *Damage Appreciation 22-23/07/41*, p. 1.

131  HO 201/9: *Damage Appreciation 18-19/07/41*, p. 1.

132  HO 201/10: *Damage Appreciation 19-20/07/41*, p. 2.

133  HO 201/10: *Damage Appreciation 19-20/07/41*, p. 3.

134  HO 201/10: *Damage Appreciation 23-24/07/41*, p. 4.

135  HO 201/10: *Damage Appreciation 23-24/07/41*, p. 1.

136  HO 201/10: *Damage Appreciation 20-21/09/41*, p. 1.

137  AN 2/1111: *D2, 18:00 12/10/41 to 06:00 13/10/41*, sheet 1.

138  HO 201/12: *Damage Appreciation 30/04-01/05/42*, p. 2.

139  AN 2/1113: *C2, 18:00 30/04/42 to 06:00 01/05/41*, sheet 1.

140  HO 201/12: *Damage Appreciation 19-20/05/42*, p. 2.

141  HO 201/12: *Damage Appreciation 19-20/05/42*, p. 1.

142  HO 201/12: *Weekly Report 13-20/05/42*, p. 2.

143  HO 201/12: *Damage Appreciation 19-20/05/42*, p. 1.

144  Ibid.

145  HO 201/13: *Damage Appreciation 30/06-01/07/42*, p. 1.

146  HO 201/13: *Damage Appreciation 30/06-01/07/42*, p. 3.

147  HO 201/13: *Damage Appreciation 30/06-01/07/42*, p. 4.

148  HO 201/13: *Damage Appreciation 24-25/10/42*, p. 1.

149  HO 201/13: *Damage Appreciation 20-21/12/42*, p. 1.

150  HO 201/14: *Damage Appreciation 03-04/01/43*, p. 1.

151  AN 2/1115: *C2, 18:00 15/01/43 to 06:00 15/02/43*, sheet 1.

152  HO 201/14: *Damage Appreciation 09-10/03/43*, p. 1.

153  HO 201/14: *Damage Appreciation 23-24/06/43*, p. 1.

154  AN 2/1116: *D2, 18:00 23/06/43 to 06:00 24/06/43*, sheet 1.

155  AN 2/1116: *D1, 06:00-18:00 24/06/43*, p. 1.

156  AN 2/1116: *D2, 18:00 24/06/43 to 06:00 25/06/43*, sheet 1.

157  HO 201/15: *Damage Appreciation 13-14/07/43*, p. 1.

158  AN 2/1116: *D2, 18:00 13/07/43 to 06:00 14/07/43*, sheet 1.

159  HO 201/15: *Damage Appreciation 13-14/07/43*, p. 1.

160  AN 2/1116: *D1, 06:00-18:00 14/07/43*, p. 1.

161  AN 2/1116: *D2, 18:00 13/07/43 to 06:00 14/07/43*, sheet 1.

162  HO 201/15: *Weekly Appreciation 07-14/07/43*, p. 4.
163  HO 201/16: *Damage Appreciation 14-15/03/44*, p. 3.
164  AN 2/1117: *RWD2, 18:00 14/03/44 to 06:00 15/03/44*, sheet 1.

## Tabula Rasa

1  Although dated as 1945, actual distribution began in 1946.
2  Abercrombie & Lutyens, 1945, plates XXIV & XXV.
3  Abercrombie & Lutyens, 1945, p. 36.
4  Abercrombie & Lutyens, 1945, p. 28.
5  *Time Flyers*, BBC2, 14 October 2003.

## Appendix 1  Fatalities In Hull Due To War Operations

1  Formerly the Hull Workhouse. Became the Western General Hospital after the formation of the NHS in 1948
2  Formerly the Sculcoates Workhouse, and sometimes listed as Beverley Road Hospital Became the Kingston General Hospital after the formation of the NHS.
3  Sometimes recorded as Hedon Road First Air Post. Site of the modern Hull Royal Infirmary.
4  Probably injured while fire-fighting at Frodsham Street.
5  Last known civilian fatality due war operations in Hull.
6  Non-air raid death – exact cause unknown.
7  Phyllis Dixon née Faulkner was married to Edwin Dixon; the brother of May Faulkner née Dixon. May was married to an Arthur Faulkner, but his relationship to Phyllis – if any – is unclear.
8  "Deaths," *Hull Daily Mail*, 04 April 1941, page 3, column 7
9  "Deaths," *Hull Daily Mail*, 04 April 1941, page 3, column 7
10  "Deaths," *Hull Daily Mail*, 02 April 1941, page 3, column 7
11  There was a raid on the night of 9/10 May, which according to Geraghty did not result in any casualties. A secret report on the heavy raids, however, states that two people were killed and three hospitalised. It has not been possible at this stage to separate the two fatalities from those of the heavy raid. HO 191/178.

12  Buried in Hull Northern Cemetery (Compt. 295, Grave 74).
13  *Supplement to the London Gazette*, 1 October 1917, page 10154.
14  Rather than being a ship, *HMS Pembroke* was the name used or a variety of shore stations. In 1941 *Pembroke I* and *Pembroke II* were accounting bases in Chatham, Kent, while *Pembroke III* was an accounting base on the Thames Estuary.
15  "Kemsing – Naval Reservist Killed," *Sevenoaks Chronicle and Kentish Advertiser*, 16 May 1941, page 4, column 2.
16  Death registered in Hull, buried in the Northern Cemetery.
17  Appears to be the daughter of Albert Dove's late wife.
18  *HMS Beaver II* was the motor launch coastal forces based at Immingham.
19  Death registered in Hull, buried in the Northern Cemetery.
20  The steam trawler *Justifier* – requisitioned as a minesweeper – was alongside in Railway Dock at the time of the raid. Fagan is buried in Hull Northern Cemetery.
21  Amy was married to Williams's son, Norman.
22  Ivy was the daughter of Hannah's daughter, Dorothy Commander née Marshall.
23  Dorothea was the daughter of Mary's daughter, Dora.
24  Buried in Upton St. Leonards (St. Leonard) Churchyard.
25  Ida was married to Ada's son, Arthur.
26  Amy was married to Alexander and Mary's son, David.
27  Eileen was the daughter of Alice's son, Lawrence Soulsby, while Eunice and Philip were the children of her daughter, Florence Wilson née Soulsby.
28  Classed as a civilian death by the CWGC, rather than Merchant Navy.
29  Classed as a civilian death by the CWGC, rather than Merchant Navy.
30  Managing director of the company.
31  Mother-in-law of Violet Burwood below.
32  Daughter-in-law of Charlotte Burwood above.
33  Married to Thomas and Mary's son, Herbert, who was serving in the Royal Artillery at the time.
34  Husband and father of Charlotte Kate Fowler and Anne Fowler, killed 13/14 April 1942.

35 Married to Mary's brother, Charles Arthur Morriss.

36 "Deaths," *Hull Daily Mail*, 12 May 1941, page 2, column 7.

37 "Deaths," *Hull Daily Mail*, 12 May 1941, page 2, column 7.

38 No raid on this date. Firth may have been injured in the raid of 8/9 May.

39 The relationship is unclear. Madge's unmarried mother appears to have died in childbirth in 1928, but there is no apparent link between her and the Airey family.

40 Buried in St. James churchyard, Sutton-on-Hull (New Yard. Row 7, Grave 2).

41 The CWGC incorrectly records this death as 8 July 1941.

42 The CWGC records this death as between 17 and 18 July 1941.

43 Buried in Hull Eastern Cemetery (Compt. 141, Grave 3).

44 The CWGC incorrectly records this death as 8 July 1941.

45 Buried in Hull Eastern Cemetery (Compt. 128, Grave 54).

46 Married to John Henry Wing (39).

47 Married to Stanley Wing (33). It is not clear how he was related to John Henry Wing, if at all.

48 The CWGC erroneously records these deaths as 27 July 1941.

49 Buried in Hull Eastern Cemetery (Compt. 289, Grave 56).

50 Married to Julia Ann's son, James Clancy, who was also serving in the Royal Navy at the time.

51 Robert appears to be the son of Julia Ann's other daughter (i.e. not Jane) by her first marriage. The CWGC erroneously dates his death as 17 August.

52 Classed as a civilian death by the CWGC, rather than Merchant Navy.

53 Geraghty erroneously dates this raid as 03 September 1941.

54 Buried in Hull Northern Cemetery (Compt. 199, Grave 36).

55 Mother of George Cavil Fowler, killed 08-09 May 1941.

56 Daughter of George Cavil Fowler, killed 08-09 May 1941.

57 *Supplement to the London Gazette*, 23 October 1918, page 3942.

58 The CWGC records the home address as 18 Bank Street, presumably in error.

59 "Deaths," Hull Daily Mail," 22 May 1942, page 4, column 9. Describes Ada and Ida as "nieces" to Edith, but the exact relationship is unclear.

60 "Family of Seven Killed," *Hull Daily Mail*, 25 May 1942, age 3, column 6. Describes King as "Uncle" to the family, but the exact relationship is unclear.

61 See Chapter 5.

62 Daughter of David and Elizabeth's daughter, Nora Elizabeth Paddison, née Walkington: "Deaths," *Hull Daily Mail*, 25 June 1943, page 2, column 9.

63 Classed as a civilian death by the CWGC, rather than Merchant Navy.

64 Appears to have been included on CWGC register due to injuries incurred whilst firewatching. See Chapter 5.

65 Appears to have been included on CWGC register due to injuries incurred during ARP duties. See Chapter 5.

66 Probably died as a result of injuries incurred during NFS duties – date and location unknown. No confirmatory inquest report can be found.

67 Buried in Hull Eastern Cemetery (Compt. 189, Grave 55).